Building Wealth Slowly

David L. Debertin

In Loving Memory of
Margaret & Harold
Debertin

Copyright © 2014 David L. Debertin

All rights reserved.

ISBN-10: 1500685747
ISBN-13: 978-1500685744

ACKNOWLEDGEMENTS

The Yahoo finance site http://finance.yahoo.com contains a wealth of information relating to how mutual funds have performed over the past ten years, including data and bar charts on the annual gains or losses for each fund for each of the last ten years. To access this, insert the ticker symbol for the fund in the "quotes" (for example VFINX), and look for the "Performance" page. This is my source of annual mutual fund data reported in the tables of this book.

The NASDAQ site http://www.nasdaq.com keeps daily historical data on individual stock prices, and separate tables containing historical dividend payments by each company. I combined data from these sources to estimate annual returns for each individual stock as reported in the individual stock tables in this book.

I would like to thank my nieces and nephew Tanya, Tamara and Kyle for providing me with many of the basic ideas I needed for they topics discussed in this book. Their assistance is greatly appreciated.

TABLE OF CONTENTS

	Preface	vi
	Ten Key Points	ix
1	An Introduction to Depreciating and Appreciating Assets	1
2	Wealth versus Income: Why They are Different	7
3	Understanding Wants and Scarcity	13
4	Motor Vehicles	20
5	Houses and Other Real Estate	29
6	Gold, Silver, Diamonds and Other Collectibles	36
7	Coping with Uncertainty	45
8	Equity Investing: the Basics	53
9	Equity Investing: Actively-Managed Funds	61
10	Equity Investing: Sector Funds	69
11	Equity Investing: Individual Stocks	82
12	Think Like an Economist!	93
13	Gathering Funds for Investment	97
14	What Every Boy and Girl (Adults Too) Should Know	107
15	America, the Beautiful	113

PREFACE

A great deal of talk is currently taking place among politicians and in the news media about the concept of *income inequality* and its possible detrimental effects on the US (and the world) economy. However, there is almost no discussion about a perhaps even larger issue, that issue being *wealth inequality*.

Income and wealth are not the same thing. Those who earn high incomes perhaps have more-and-better *opportunities* to *build* wealth, but many do not. We have all watched as many high-income people with out-of-control spending habits live on the very *edge* of going bankrupt. Then we hear stories of people with comparatively low incomes who died and surprisingly left estates worth many millions of dollars. Then stories emerge that many if not most multimillion-dollar lottery winners end up bankrupt by making a series of unwise choices with respect to managing the money they won.

What gives, anyway? The basis for this book is a simple idea: wealth-building is at least as much about how individuals choose to *spend* the money they earn as it is about *how much* they earn. People with good incomes who have no wealth almost invariably choose spending patterns that focus on buying things that depreciate, rather than appreciate in value. The basic problem is not just a single unwise choice, bit a long series of choices in spending for immediate gratification rather than building a long-term asset-and-wealth position.

Successful wealth-building requires a combination of *discipline, courage* and *patience. Discipline* is needed to *forego consumption* and to forego using funds to *buy depreciating assets* in order to instead have the money necessary to *buy assets that might* appreciate over the long term.

Courage focuses on making choices from an array of potentially-appreciating assets, even though these assets lose money for a significant period of time. In particular, this involves *not being afraid* to do the opposite of what everyone else seems to be doing.

Patience is needed in order to deal with investment situations that sometimes go against you. Oftentimes, price declines are instead buying opportunities in disguise. Most of the time, the best way to deal with a *paper loss* of money is to simply stay invested, and not try to sell out at the lower price. This book is not about schemes for getting rich quickly: It is about building wealth slowly over a sustained period of time.

Television ads tell us this over and over. The nation's economy is collapsing! Federal debt is out of control as a direct consequence of politicians vying to outdo each other by giving voters an assortment of "free" stuff. The Federal Reserve bank is printing money as if tomorrow will never come. Are you better off putting your funds in gold coins and storing them in a bank safety-deposit box, or would you be better off with the equivalent investment in common stock in the food company General Mills?

Real estate seems like an excellent way to build wealth. The value of farmland appears to be increasing all the time, and the stock market is always moving but you never know where, up, down, sideways. You never know what tomorrow might bring in the stock market. I cannot live in an equity fund, but I can live in a nice house. That is a key advantage of a house over a mutual fund. Which is better, a nice house or the equivalent investment in an fund investing in stocks? How about those farmers that own farmland? Are they gradually getting rich?

Other people somehow seem to have all the good luck. They latch on to stuff that usually appears to increase not decrease in value over time. The things I buy seems to always go down not up in value over time. How come I do not have the *good luck* other people seem to have? I buy lottery tickets, but it always seems that other people win, not me. For goodness sakes, what is wrong with me? When is the sun going to shine on me too?

I see my lot in life is making sure my children have it much. I want to make sure my children have all the stuff that I did not have when I was their age. I am there to provide them the opportunity to *have a good childhood*. This view, in turn, leads to spending habits that focus on using money for spending on stuff for *immediate gratification* rather than for *wealth building*. A position in a mutual fund looks quite boring compared to a trip to Disney World. Do you really think funds in a stock mutual fund is more important in my life than the expensive Disney World trip? Or perhaps is there a reasonable path that could make both happen?

I do not provide you with definitive answers to any of these questions. Instead, I will show you some information and numbers that address each of these issues, and each of you *can then reach your own conclusion* as to what is best for your particular situation.

TEN KEY POINTS

1. Media attention has been focusing on income inequality. Wealth inequality is even more extreme. Income and wealth are linked, but they are not the same thing.
2. Building wealth can be as much about changing spending habits as it is about finding more income. Many people who fail to build wealth allocate too great a portion of their incomes to buying things that will always depreciate in value rather than seeking investments that may increase in value.
3. Building wealth requires a person to defer current consumption if an effort to pursue future gains, and requires a combination of discipline, courage, patience and determination.
4. Most people hate to have anyone be critical with respect to how they spend their money. You could easier tell them that their dog isn't pretty!
5. Assets that possibly appreciate in value usually do not steadily go up. Learning to live with short-term price fluctuations (volatility) is part of learning how to build wealth.
6. Being able to determine what is a reasonable risk versus an unreasonable risk (such as a lottery ticket) in wealth-building is important.
7. Strategies exist which make wealth-building using the stock market fairly easy, assuming you can get your head around and deal with the volatility.

8. There are always people buying stocks when they should be selling, or selling stocks when they should be buying. Most people hate losing money, but they have a tough time resisting a rapidly-increasing share price.
9. Buying motor vehicles has made a lot of people broke who could have been wealthy.
10. A dollar you spend today on something that does not appreciate in value is a dollar you will never be able to spend in the future.

Chapter 1

An Introduction to Depreciating and Appreciating Assets

> **Question 1**: *What have you purchased recently that has appreciated or likely will be appreciating in value?*
>
> **Question 2**: *What have you purchased or recently that is now worth less than you paid for it?*

If your answer to question 1 is *"nothing"* or *"almost nothing"*, that means your answer to question 2 has to be *"everything"* or *"almost everything."* This also means that your financial planning skills need some work, and that is putting it mildly!

The two key words here are *"discipline"* and *"courage"*. What is discipline? Discipline involves, first, admitting that not all goods which decline in value over time are so important in your life that there is never any room in your budget to make purchases of goods that have appreciation potential over a long period. The wealthy and the non-wealthy differ substantially in this regard. Not only do the wealthy allocate a *higher proportion* of their incomes to goods that usually *appreciate in value* over time, something else interesting from an economic perspective happens.

As a general rule, the wealthy derive *satisfaction* (a economist might instead say *utility*) not only from goods that depreciate in value over time, they might actually derive even *more satisfaction* from seeing money grow without ever spending it, in other words, there is satisfaction (utility) that comes about from seeing the equivalent of $2 where only $1 used to be.

Everyone is different in this regard. Some people are so obsessed with having lots of rapidly-depreciating goods from Target® or from the local auto dealership, they accumulate ever-increasing amounts of debt. If these people do that, they certainly are not going to have any money to buy goods that could perhaps (or likely will) appreciate in value, and they will spend their lives complaining about how broke they are and then how the world has always mistreated them from a financial perspective.

This is called *living in the short-term* or *as if tomorrow will never come*. There is no point in accumulating stuff that could be worth more tomorrow, because we will never get to tomorrow. This attitude is a financially-irresponsible approach to life, and it's a good way of ensuring that you will always wake up every morning being miserable as you worry about how sorry your finances are.

Discipline is mainly about *foregoing some possible current consumption* in search of *larger future gains*. If you are convinced that the future will not happen, then there is no point in being concerned about what the future might hold, and with that what your wealth position might be once you get there. But always living in the present with no concern for the future can be quite miserable strategy for life.

Discipline definitely does not *involve going hungry*. Instead, discipline is about continually making a series of *wise choices* over a long period of time. Generally, these are choices that *save money* in the present, and thus *leave more money* for investment in *appreciating assets*. At the grocery, maybe the store brand *tastes better* than the national brand and *costs less* too. Maybe you can find perfectly-adequate clothes from Walmart® or K mart®, and add the money you saved to your fund for *buying assets that will potentially appreciate*.

These may appear to be *small items* for sure, but the nickels and dimes that are saved in making each of these *wise choices* add up over time, and the accumulating nickels and dimes when invested properly over time build wealth. An important *first step* in building wealth is to sweat the choices involving the *little stuff*, the stuff the non-wealthy think *are items too small to even matter*. In wealth-building, *everything matters*!

A *bigger concern* is that many people spend too much money *buying and feeding motor vehicles*. The saving from going a more frugal route can add up quickly. Excessive spending on motor vehicles is a major reason why most people are unable to achieve wealth. I feel so strongly about the issues people frequently have in this regard that I am devoting an entire chapter to that topic.

The second word is "courage." This is the other major characteristic most people lack and a *second basic reason* why there are *fewer wealthy people than non-wealthy people*. I have done financial counseling for people who are contemplating making purchases of assets that have *appreciation potential*, whether they be *financial assets* such as stocks and bonds or *other potentially-appreciating assets* such as real estate.

There are several issues here. First, every asset with appreciation potential also has *some potential to decline*, perhaps for *successive years* at a time. A lot of people seek *risk-free investments that consistently appreciate at a substantial pace.* These options, that is, a series of risk-free options which also appreciate rapidly, do not exist. If you restrict yourself only to those investments that will never decline in value, you will be dealing with a very short list. Some people never achieve any wealth because *they refuse to take on any risk at all.* That strategy never works.

But it also does not work to use the *I don't like take any risk argument* as an excuse to *never* make an investment in an appreciating asset but only buy assets that depreciate from a store such as Target® or at the local automobile dealership, either. As a wealth-creation strategy, claiming that *making any investment for the future is too risky for me* is a lame excuse.

The second thing the non-wealthy often do with abandon is to take on risk where the probability of appreciation is so low that, as a practical matter it, is nonexistent. The classic example is *buying a lottery ticket.* These are outside bets, not serious investments. Of course, someone *will* win the lottery, but chances are it will not be you!

The appreciating assets investment "sweet spot" clearly lies somewhere in the middle, that is, *between the two extremes* of taking on the lottery-ticket risk versus never putting money in anything more risky than a checking account. Even the investors who believe they are the best at this can get fooled. I have gone into financial investments that appear to be all but perfect, providing a *9 percent historical rate-of-return consistently for a dozen years (or more).* Once I got in, the investment *promptly tanked* and showed a negative return. I persevered.

This brings up the next topic, another thing the wealthy do differently from the non-wealthy. The average

An Introduction to Depreciating and Appreciating Assets

individual buying an investment where the appreciation rate *moves from positive to negative and back again* (volatility) tends to want to *purchase when prices are soaring*, and *sell when prices are plummeting*. Oftentimes, the wealthy have a *different scheme* in mind. Strategically, they like *buy* when prices are tanking, and *sell* when prices are soaring. The wealthy *hate* to pay full price for *anything*!

Fundamentally, the *truly wealthy are non-stop cheapskates*. But more importantly, they don't let *shorter-run price declines* in a usually-appreciating asset affect their longer-term *decision making*. Investing when others are fleeing can be fun for a disciplined, wealth-seeking investor. There are so many people heading to the exits when a stock drops sharply that you can sometimes have a lot of fun playing the contrarian by putting in "buy" bids when everyone else is getting out. This is not a technique I would necessarily recommend for the first-time stock-market investor to try. In part, you need to first seriously study whether the company investors are fleeing is in real danger of going bankrupt, in which case you lose your entire investment. (This is something better attempted with stock in Best Buy® than with Blockbuster® stock!)

In summary, the basic reasons why most people do not accumulate wealth are

> 1. A preoccupation with living life in the present as opposed to a serious interest and concern for what the *future might hold*.

> 2. A preoccupation with always trying to own the best (even if it costs a lot more) and making purchases at the most expensive places. The best often is not really any better, but merely the most heavily advertized.

3. Being absolutely convinced that small savings accomplished on a daily basis never will amount to anything important or significant over time.

4. Failure to assess risks versus rewards objectively. This leads to making "investments" in buying lottery tickets rather than in the stock market.

5. An inability to have the *courage* to invest in assets that have good odds of appreciating over time given that there is some chance that each investment will head south. If you lack the courage to have money in anything other than a bank checking or savings account, you suffer from this problem.

6. Lacking the *discipline* to forego some current consumption in order to build funds to purchase potentially appreciating assets

7. Lacking the willingness to purchase potentially-appreciating assets when others are selling and prices for getting in are low by historical standards.

Chapter 2

Wealth versus Income: Why They are Different

Many people think of wealth as being the same as income, but the two concepts are completely different. Part of the reason for the confusion is that people see the wealthy as being people who have high incomes, but the non-wealthy are those who have low incomes.

So, the first question I need to address is "what is income?" Most people think of income as the wages or salaries that they earn while being employed by someone else. Income in this context is the *reward* for doing hard and complicated work. Then, the amount of income a person has determines *how much* that person can spend, usually on *depreciating* assets. High-income people have more things than low-income people, or so the argument goes.

In reality, however, many people do not earn income primarily from wages and salaries, and there are many income sources that cannot reasonably be called a wage or a salary. Indeed, a person's income might include some money from wages and salaries, but most of the money could come from other sources. For example, an ex-politician might give speeches to groups to earn income. An owner of rental property might obtain income from the rents obtained from the property. A book-writer might get income from royalties in the sale of books, and so on.

The concept of wealth is closely linked to the ownership of appreciating assets, or at least assets that appreciate in value in most years, if not in every year. Using this measure, many people who have high incomes are not wealthy. There is nothing to stop a high-income person from spending all income on assets that quickly depreciate, and many high-income people do.

We all have encountered high-income people who seem to be on the very brink of (perhaps yet another) financial disaster. These people blow money on fancy cars, expensive vacations and on other items that quickly lose value, if not disappear entirely. An *expensive trip* to Disney World® may be fun, but it is *anything but a wealth-creation strategy*. After the trip is over, there is nothing that remains of the income that was spent on the trip. If one seeks to acquire wealth, such a trip is a particularly bad thing to do, as it quickly turns the income into something of zero value. I suppose pleasant memories are worth *something* to one's psyche, but no one ever became wealthy by packing up and going to Disney World®!

I suspect that the odds of a low-income person becoming wealthy via the purchase and ownership of appreciating assets is lower than the odds of a high-income person becoming wealthy via the same ownership of appreciating assets, because, at least in theory, the high-income person probably has *fewer demands* on income for the purchase of depreciating assets than does the low-income person.

I hesitate to make a lot of generalizations here, however, on how high-income people behave, because I have watched many high-income people who are in a low-wealth situation in large measure because they refused to make purchases of anything but rapidly-depreciating assets. Conversely, I have watched many people of but modest means continue to siphon income *away from rapidly-depreciating goods* into assets that broadly appreciate in value. We have all heard examples of people of only modest income who had giant estates because they made wise choices focusing on the purchase of *assets that usually appreciate in value* over time.

Life-lesson for today and tomorrow: Wealthy people are not necessarily smarter or luckier than non-wealthy people. It is just that wealthy people become wealthy by focusing on accumulating assets that are likely to appreciate not depreciate over time. Wealthy people sometimes might be *braver* and have more *courage* than non-wealthy people, however.

Your *income* is the *sum* of all the money that came to you during the year that is *potentially subject to federal and state income taxes*. You calculate your exact income each time you fill out an income tax return.

Your *wealth* is calculated by *summing the current market value of everything you own* including the current market value of your depreciating and appreciating assets. From this value is *subtracted any money you owe others*. Examples of money owed to others include home mortgages, car loans and credit card debt. What is left technically is your *net worth*, a direct measure of your *wealth*.

Your *net-worth number* is likely very different from the *income number* you reported to the Internal Revenue Service. Your net worth could be higher or lower than your annual income. If your net worth is significantly lower than your annual income, you are decidedly non-wealthy and you need to examine your spending habits. To the extent that your net worth is higher than your annual income, you are at least on your way to *accumulating wealth*.

The US tax system is heavily tilted toward taxing *income* rather than *wealth*. One exception to this is real estate and sometimes personal property taxes, but these are normally levied by states and municipalities, not the federal government. For the most part, however, accumulated wealth is left untaxed by the federal government until the asset is sold, when the net proceeds from the sale enter the income stream. Another exception is estate taxes. If a person dies, federal and state estate taxes are based on the current asset value. However, unless a person dies, wealth accumulates tax-deferred. The living wealthy pay none or minimal taxes to the US government on the *unrealized appreciation* in the value of assets.

Current federal and state income tax laws makes it comparatively easy to *build wealth* over time, and this is a tax break the *wealthy routinely employ* to easily achieve more wealth. All that is required to take advantage of federal tax laws is the *courage* to assume the risks involved and the *discipline* to be willing to forego some current consumption in order to buy assets with appreciation potential.

Oddly, discussions about income inequality almost invariably end with discussions relating to how the top marginal tax rates on high-income earners should be made higher. No mention is made with respect to the Federal government taxing *wealth* as assets appreciate. Of course, broadly speaking, investments made in appreciating assets lead to economic growth and move the nation's economy forward. Taxing unrealized gains could quickly slow the economic growth rate. Neither political party advocates the federal taxation of the unrealized appreciation of assets as a strategy for reducing inequality within the masses.

Many people who are not wealthy like to think that the wealthy people they see around them somehow just *got lucky*. While *dumb luck* can be a component of acquiring wealth, the wealthy are often very good at *setting up the preconditions necessary* so that dumb luck can occur. They are also good at sizing up odds, and separating the *reasonable* odds of winning from the *near-impossible* odds of winning. Think of a lottery ticket as an example.

We do not normally see the *wealthy lined up at convenience stores to buy lottery tickets*. The reason, of course, is that they have taken a look at the odds of winning (or even getting back just the cost of the ticket) and concluded that purchasing the lottery ticket likely will destroy, not create wealth. Lottery-ticket buyers generally are people of but modest means, people who mistakenly believe that something with near zero odds of occurring will happen to them.

At the same time, becoming wealthy nearly always involves assuming *some* risk in a situation where outcomes are uncertain. If the odds were 100 percent, the returns in terms of potential asset appreciation would be minimal. The non-wealthy are often uncomfortable in laying out money to purchase an asset when outcomes, even over the longer term, are uncertain. This frequently becomes an *excuse for spending money* on something that will *surely depreciate* over time.

An example would be the choice of spending $20,000 on a stock versus $20,000 on a new car. The stock *could* decline in value over the next five years: the odds are *all but certain* that the new car will decline in value over the same period of time. The *possibility* that the stock could decline in value *drives the decision to purchase* the new car instead! Further, no one will know if a person purchased the stock, but everyone in the neighborhood will know the same person has the new car.

This is where the courage and discipline come in. The new car is certainly fun to drive: The stock is just there, and no one in the neighborhood can see it. It certainly takes *discipline* to opt for the stock over the new car, in particular, discipline which requires that a person forego current consumption in an attempt to acquire wealth.

This also takes a lot of *courage*. The new car will deliver a *stream of services* over perhaps a period of five or more years. You can go places and do things in the car. Goodness, you could even drive to Disney World® in it! The stock could easily *double or triple in value*, if you picked the right stock at the right price. But the stock could also *halve in value*, too. A lot of people rationalize buying the car over the stock simply because they are put off by the possibility that the stock could go down in value. The car will fall apart too, eventually, but that does not seem to bother them.

Chapter 3

Understanding Wants and Scarcity

In my opening remarks on the first day of class for incoming freshmen in applied economics, I would say

> *"Economics is all about recognizing two basic ideas. First, human wants are unlimited. Second, the means to fulfill these wants are always limited, no matter how much money you have. So economics involves making* **wise** *choices, specifically identifying the* **specific choices** *that will* **best fulfill the unlimited wants** *using only* **scarce resources** *to acquire them."*

There is no better illustration of the practical problems people face in dealing with these issues than the issue of *spending right now* for current consumption by buying goods that almost always depreciate in value over time versus *deferring spending* with the idea of reaping future gains in wealth by acquiring assets that likely will appreciate in value.

No one ever said that this was going to be an easy choice to make. There is always stuff out there that anyone would like to own. A shiny car now is a lot more interesting than the same amount of money invested in a tax-deferred Individual Retirement Account. But maybe the motor vehicle is not the wise choice. A lot of people might chose the shiny car because they are not convinced that the long-term investment will pay off.

I have never determined why so many people get so hung up on owning assets that will soon become worthless. It makes no sense at all. Usually, I want to stand up and scream in protest! Why are you doing these dumb things? Of course, I am the one who thinks they are dumb.

Financial planning conflicts often are a source of conflict in relationships between partners. I have read that financial conflicts come in second only to issues relating to sex in marital conflicts, and for many the financial conflicts are more important than the conflicts involving sex.

There are three ways this could go down. First, both partners could be fixated on *the ownership of depreciating assets*. They stick it out together but spend their lives careening from one financial crisis to another. No matter how much money they have, there is always something else out there they would *really like to have*. In buying stuff, they go from one financial crisis to another, accumulating lots of credit card and other debt as they go along. Then soon, the refrigerator goes out, and there is not any money in the bank account to get a new one. The new refrigerator just adds to the credit-card debt, and a continuously deteriorating, not improving, standard of living. Credit-card debt is a certain path to having an ever lower, not higher standard of living.

You get the idea. As the accumulated debt builds, the couple frequently ends up leaning on other family members to bail them out of the latest crisis. These people think they have an income problem, when in reality, they have a spending problem. They are unwilling to defer consumption, not alter their spending patterns to make less-costly choices. It is important to own the *best of everything*, all bought on credit or not.

Second, a common situation is where one partner is hung up on owning rapidly-depreciating assets, but the other partner wants to defer at least some current consumption in favor of a potential long-term gain. In the world of partner relationships, this is a relationship akin to a raging fire. When any unallocated income comes in, it is like throwing gasoline on the raging fire. There is an immediate fight over what should be done with it. One partner wants to *buy something*, and the other may want to *invest* the money.

There is no rule that says which partner is going to play each part in the drama. Farm couples frequently get into this one. The man wants *some fancy new piece of farm equipment*, such as a combine with a Global Positioning System. The farm wife thinks the house is falling apart and needs to be remodeled. Either of these *could* be a good long-term investment. Neither one of them is *blowing money* on *depreciating assets*. The farmer *might* be able to make more money from the farm with the fancy new equipment.

The farm wife *might* increase the value of the home over the long term. But a lot of the *features on new combines* are not unlike other *boy toys*. The farmer can *easily* get carried away with expensive stuff that is fun but does not significantly improve the profitability of the farm. The farm wife could easily get carried away too. In an urban area the conflict sometimes arises as to whether the money should be spent on boy toys versus girl toys (girls have toys too, toys that big boys care little about).

For decades, my department struggled with the issue as to why two farmers both with similar farms could have such drastically different annual profits. The basic conclusion has usually been that the farmer with the highest profits had far *better control over costs and expenses*. the argument that the new boy-toy combine with a host of interesting and costly features is somehow also a profit-maximizing strategy goes out the door.

Third, both partners believe in deferring some consumption for the sake of long-term gain. There may be conflicts with respect to the type of appreciating asset, but everyone is generally on the same financial page. A new house could appreciate in value, but so could the money invested in the stock market. I have seen both the upside and downside potential of both.

I cannot draw any general conclusions. Long term, the stock market overall appreciates in about the 10-11 percent annual range. Nationally, houses appreciate long-term in the 3-5 percent range. At first, the stock market seems to have a wide edge. But there are many examples of people who bought houses recently at high prices in the mistaken belief that *prices will never fall*, but quickly ended up with a house worth only *half as much* as they paid. Or, maybe, *twice as much*. You just never know.

A house always provides a place to live. Economists refer to this as a stream of *imputed* rents. You cannot live in a stock market investment. Further, home appreciation accumulates on a tax-deferred basis if at all ($500,000 couple's exemption from tax on the sale, $250,000 for a single person). This can be trickier in stock market investments. From a relationship perspective, the couple's focus on making decisions that might have big payoffs in the longer term becomes a generally-happy situation.

Nowadays, crass materialism is so rampant in the US that sometimes I just want to scream in protest. The problems here are twofold. A lot of people are *dissatisfied* with anything but the *biggest meal at the fast-food joint*. People are unhappy if they don't drive a *fancy SUV*. People want to wear only *name-brand clothes* purchased at a fancy department store. Clothes bought at Walmart® are just not good enough any more.

All of this violates a large number of *rules* I have lived by throughout my life, never mind that the admonitions against this kind of behavior at the core of religious values focusing on the downside of *excessive materialism*. Throwing more money at people engaged in crass materialism is like throwing gasoline on an already-raging fire. Buying expensive things shows a *contempt for basic Christian values*. A lot of what the Pope is saying is right, especially about the dangers in crass materialism with the emphasis on consuming more in all sorts of ways. I would disagree with him on some issues, but this one he has down, exactly.

I had a really interesting time growing up. The lessons I learned were invaluable. Dad always had some piece of farm equipment he wanted to own. Sometimes whatever he was thinking of was within his means but often not. Mom and dad got along very well, at least 98 percent of the time. Mom had things she wanted too, but never did her wants get in the way of what dad wanted to do so long as she felt that what dad was doing would help *make the farm better* over the longer haul.

I often think about that pair. I do not recall my mom driving a tractor, ever. That was dad's job. She did a lot of other useful and important things all around the farm, feeding the bottle lambs, taking care of the livestock etc, but she did not ever actually drive a tractor. But she was the financial "brains" of the operation. Never mind that computers had not been invented yet, she had a computer in her head. Her TurboTax® software was in her head. It was just amazing to watch her when she was at her peak. Dad did the farming and mom did the financial management.

It was equally fun to see both of them operate in front of a farm credit agency (Production Credit Association or PCA in those days). In the space of about five minutes she had wowed the credit officers, and dad had the credit he needed to farm for another year. Mom knew exactly where every dollar was going. The farm credit people were so wowed by her prowess that the annual meetings at the PCA kept getting shorter and shorter. Dad could not operate without my mom's financial skills, but my mom could not have operated without my dad, either.

Understanding Wants and Scarcity

On a personal level, I was pleased to discover that somehow I managed to inherit the genes I wanted from both my parents. From my mom, I got a few numerical, computer and related financial-management skills which I tried to improve upon on my own. I developed a real interest in specific techniques needed to build long-term wealth instead of immediate consumption not only as a career but as an overall strategy for life. I also developed a long list of strategies for saving money when, as a last resort, depreciating assets *had* to be purchased.

Over time, I got good at it. My mom was always deeply fearful of taking significant risks of any kind. Dad always ran a little further out on the edge. He was the risk-taker in the family. I got my risk-taking ability directly from my dad not my mom, and I am also very thankful for that and how the two sets of skills could be successfully meshed in a professional career in applied economics. From my parents, I got both a career that served me well, but more importantly an entire way of life! Along the way, I added a few touches all my own that neither of my parents had considered.

Chapter 4

Motor Vehicles

What about motor vehicles? I have been thinking about long-term appreciation rates on 1969 Camaros, since I happen to own one that I purchased new in 1969. Some of you may appreciate that the 1969 Camaro might be the all-time most popular collector car in existence. I paid $2,900 for mine, in February, 1969 as measured in 1969 dollars. On a good day, it *might* be worth $30,000 in 2014. That may seem like an excellent rate of appreciation, but in the process of getting it there I have probably spent close to $20,000 in repairs and body work over the years. And I did get to drive the car for nearly 9 years, so the "investment" was not a complete bust.

However, the $2,900 invested in any number of stocks would have been worth a whole lot more. And I have had to worry about storing the dumb thing for a long period of time even to get to this point. And keep in mind that a dollar in 1969 was worth a lot more than a dollar today.

So, the great majority of vehicles coming out of a dealership fall in the category of a *nearly-certain depreciating asset* not an asset that is likely to ever appreciate in value. An easy thing to do is to count the doors. If the vehicle has four not two doors it is 99.99 percent certain that it will be a *depreciating asset* if held over a long period of time. The Camaro is 45 years old. Are you interested in holding a vehicle for 45 years and making a bet that you picked the right vehicle when you made your initial purchase to check this all out?

Part of the problem is that in order to make money holding a vehicle as a potential collectible, it has to have only two doors. Better still if the top comes down. How many new vehicles are being manufactured currently with only two doors? For that matter, how many convertibles are currently being manufactured?

Interestingly, I am testing some of these theories, as I also have a vehicle with 2 doors that is now near 20 years old, a 1995 Chrysler Sebring coupe. When the 1969 Camaro became 20 years old in 1989, its value was starting to appreciate in value and collector interest in the vehicle. Not so with the Sebring, at least not yet. Likely, never!

The Sebring body is almost as perfect as a new vehicle would be, and it runs like a top. It has acquired 67,000 miles in 20 years. It has the proper 2 doors. It cost $18,000 new in 1995, but in 1995 dollars. On a really good day, it *might* today be worth $1,500. What gives? I am certainly not going to build wealth hanging on to a 1995 Sebring coupe.

Over the years, I've owned a number of other motor vehicles, all with the proper number of doors (2) to be a potential long-term collectible (appreciating asset), or so I thought when I made the purchase. I held on to each of them for varying lengths of time, but then sold them. The next car was a bright firethorn metallic red 1977 Camaro, purchased new for $5,600. By then, I was employed as a college professor, and doing consulting work in Indianapolis, Indiana, some 200 miles away. I had become concerned about the potential reliability of the 69 Camaro, which was starting to show its age.

The 77 Camaro was never really the right car for the consulting trips. It was rear-wheel drive and tended to slide around on slippery roads, although not quite as badly as the 69 Camaro had. I was driving 200 miles to Indianapolis all times of the year.

What about one of these new-fangled front-wheel-drive vehicles? General Motors had a new line of front wheel drive vehicles in 1980, the Chevy Citation, Pontiac Phoenix, Oldsmobile Omega and the Buick Skylark. The problem was that I wanted to order the Buick version, which was the most expensive, and it was going to be $8,100. In the winter of 1979-80 I sold the Camaro to a colleague (for only $2,500), and ordered the Buick Skylark in the exact color and with the exact equipment I wanted.

By then I had determined that, first, I needed tax write-offs to deduct from my increasing consulting income, and second, I really was not using my car to drive anywhere of any distance other than for consulting work. Some quick calculations allowed me to write off two-thirds of the cost of the vehicle as depreciation expense against my consulting income. So the federal government ended up paying for quite a bit of the cost of the Buick by reducing the tax bill I would have paid otherwise.

As a car, the Buick Skylark was my least favorite of those I have ever owned. I kept it until the fall of 1986, a long time compared to the quick sale of the 1977 firethorn red Camaro. The Buick managed to blow its radiator after only about 4 years of ownership, and as a consequence blew its head gasket. I am not fond of the 60-degree GM V6 block introduced that year, which became the block for the entire "high value" line of V6 engines GM stopped building only recently. My version was a V6 with only 2.8 liters, but that soon became the 3.1 liter version and then the 3.5 and 3.9 liter versions.

Maybe the basic problem with that engine was that I just had the earliest version, but the car still had other serious issues. The car moved forward ok on slick roads, but you had to remember to never step on the brakes if the roads were icy. I did that once on a slick day and the car did a full 180 degrees and ended up in the opposite lane going completely in the other direction. I was just lucky that there was no oncoming traffic that day.

The problem was that the rear drum brakes were taken from a smaller GM vehicle and were way too small for the weight of the V6 engine, so that when I braked on slippery roads the front wheels locked and the rear end of the car rotated around the weight of the engine like the handle of a sledge hammer.

This is one of those instances where GM executives insisted that there was nothing inherently wrong with the vehicle design or the design or size of the rear drums. In reality, GM did not want to address what would have been a very costly recall to upgrade the rear brakes in all the V6 cars using that chassis, nor face the lawsuits from all of the accidents that were happening because of the 180s the car did on even slightly-slippery roads. Then there were the body issues, as in water that leaked through the front windshield molding and on to the dash.

I drove the Buick to Florida one year, but it was warm and sunny and the wheels stayed planted on the road and the windshield didn't leak water. I sold it to a colleague in 1986 ($1,500, 47,000 miles) and he promptly had more problems with it too, starting with a gimpy key lock that failed on the first day he owned it. He eventually sold the car to a graduate student, who drove it into a deer. I thought it was good to get it off the road!

At that point I bought the 1986 Subaru XT coupe ($11,000 in an all-cash deal). The Subaru XT coupe was known for its eccentric (some would say weird) styling. The Subaru was a better car than the Buick, but was not trouble-free either. The car was odd in appearance, and odd things broke. I spent $300 to repair the stalk dimmer switch and $400 to fix a non-working horn. The 4-cylinder boxer had only 96 horsepower and was noisy and coarse. This was not my favorite engine and I vowed never again to own another 4-cylinder. I sold the Subaru in a private sale for $3500 in 1995, not a bad price, in retrospect.

Of the cars after the 1969 Camaro, the only one that currently has some collector interest was the firethoirn red 1977 Camaro. Camaros from the mid and late 1970s are being restored, and prices for these cars are moving upward, although still not nearly where the prices for late 1960s Camaros are.

The entire collector car market is interesting in that there is always lots of interest in 2-door cars built on the 1950s and 60s. There are fewer collector cars built in the 1970s, with most of them being coupes and convertibles from the early 1970s. The Camaro is one of only a few cars from the mid-to-late 70s with significant collector interest.

The year 1980 marks the end of the collectible cars market, with a few oddball exceptions from the 1980s such as the DeLorean. Some Corvettes from the 1980s and 90s are at least maintaining their value. If you purchase a vehicle from the 1980s or 90s with the idea that it could become an appreciating collectible, good luck, as the odds of being successful at this are very low.

The motor vehicles of all types being made-and-sold today have all but zero probability of appreciating in value over time. You might discover that a particular vehicle holds its value better than another vehicle, but that is about it. The vehicles being sold today in any numbers are *appliances* that provide a service, much like an electric range or refrigerator provide services. The best of the new vehicles provide a service reliably, with few issues and problems.

Certainly most people do not buy motor vehicles and plan to hang on to them for 20 years with the thought that they will become collectible by then and appreciate in value. I have gotten to drive the Sebring for 20 years and received back a stream of services in transportation. But if you obsess on buying vehicles frequently you are likely going to manage to make yourself poor not wealthy! Since buying motor vehicles is an effective method for making sure that you never become wealthy.

If you want to try and build wealth in the collector car market, feel free to do so, but this is a very specialized business that usually takes specialized knowledge in order to succeed. A better strategy for most people is to spend as little money as possibly can on vehicles and use all the money saved to purchase assets that have better odds of appreciating in value! Here are some strategies for saving money on vehicles.

1. *If an all possible, pay cash for motor vehicles.* This will keep you from buying more vehicle than you can truly afford, and save you substantial sums of money in interest charges over the life of the vehicle. If you cannot afford to pay cash perhaps you need to look for a less expensive vehicle.
2. *Drive vehicles until the wheels fall off, or nearly so.* Many people go into frequent vehicle trading on the grounds that the newer, lower-mileage vehicle will be more reliable. I guess they worry that the older vehicle will more likely break down and

leave them stranded on the side of the road. Yet, the empirical evidence for this is not strong. Do you see many 10-year-old vehicles stranded on the side of the road? Are the odds of getting stranded really any greater in a 10-year old vehicle than in a 3-year old vehicle? Think about that. Do not just assume that you somehow *need* to trade vehicles every three or four years.

3. *Try to let the other guy pay the initial depreciation, if possible.* Dig through the slightly-used as opposed to the new-car showroom. The depreciation on a vehicle is highest in the first two or three years of ownership. Bargains can often be found among cars coming off two- and three-year leases. Shoot for a vehicle with under 30,000 miles and a price about 50 percent of what the vehicle would have sold for new.

4. *The best deals are often on 2-3 year old vehicles that were less than completely successful in the marketplace.* For example, low-mileage two- and three-year old Toyota Camrys and Honda Accords always bring a premium price in the "slightly-used" marketplace, the two companies both having a strong reputation for building reliable vehicles. A slightly less-sought-after vehicle such as a Nissan Altima or a Mazda 626 might very well be largely ignored by used car buyers, and thus have a lower slightly-used price. Dealers know which brands and models tend to attract customers and price the used versions of these vehicles accordingly. The less-sought-after brand might be in better condition with lower miles for the same money you would pay just to drive the more sought-after brand! You obviously do not want to buy a brand with reliability issues, but often a less-sought-after brand is at least as reliable as a more-sought-after brand.

5. *Buying a vehicle brand with a higher annual depreciation rate rather than a lower depreciation rate might be a money-saving tactic, for three reasons.* First, if you plan to drive the vehicle till the wheels fall off, its residual value will be under $1,000 anyway. Second, if you live in a state that taxes vehicles as personal property, you will save on taxes in each year of ownership. Third, a factor in determining auto insurance rates is the current value of the vehicle, and you may save on auto insurance over time if you buy the vehicle with the faster depreciation rate.

Spending excessive amounts of money on expensive motor vehicles by either leasing or buying on credit is a major impediment to building wealth over the long term. This money is nearly always money that could better be siphoned off to purchase assets with far better odds of appreciating in value.

In purchasing vehicles first ask yourself "why am I buying this at all?" If this is a second (or third) vehicle, is this really needed? A vehicle is a lot like a pet. It is not only the initial cost, but the care and feeding, that is, the gasoline, insurance and repairs and which must be covered in your budget. These dollars could be better employed by buying an asset with far better odds of appreciating unless you simply enjoy throwing money into the wind!

Second, what features do you really *need* in the vehicle, as opposed to merely *want*? Are heated and cooled seats really necessary for you to exist? Leather upholstery? A sunroof? GPS? Dealers love to see customers coming in who demand these items as they are the real *profit-centers* for the dealership. Do you really want to limit your ability to build wealth over the long term simply because you have discovered that you cannot somehow live without the latest vehicle doodad! If you really think that somehow life as you want it to be would somehow end without the doodad, maybe it is time to look for a vehicle with the particular feature among the slightly-used models, where you will pay substantially less for the feature, if at all.

Third, is owning this vehicle going to allow you to make more income, or is it merely a convenience? If the latter, might you be able to live without it entirely.

To conclude, the ownership of excessive numbers of depreciating, gadget-laden leased or purchased-on-credit vehicles is perhaps the *single most important impediment to building wealth* over time. Motor vehicles are *wealth-destroyers, not wealth-creators*. Feeling that you somehow always have to buy new is a serious problem, as is the care and feeding of vehicles that you do not really need. Think of motor vehicles as much like giant vacuum cleaners that suck up cash that could be deployed for better building real wealth.

Chapter 5

Houses and Other Real Estate

Residential real estate, that is, houses, for most people is the largest category of personal wealth. If the average person were to construct a net-worth statement, probably the largest item on the "assets" side would be the value of the owned (and probably mortgaged) house.

Unlike most assets with appreciation potential, houses not only frequently appreciate in value, but also provide a stream of services over time. (Economists call this stream of services *imputed rents* for good reason. If a house were not owned, then the person or family would likely be renting housing instead.) The combination of being able to live in a house along with at least the possibility of appreciation potential is very attractive, and a major issue can be that people *over*invest in residential real estate as an asset-building strategy rather than *under*invest.

As potentially-appreciating assets, houses can be very tricky indeed. If I were to look at national averages for residential homes, I would discover that the average annual appreciation rate over 20 years or more is probably in the 3- to 5-percent-per-year range. This is a fairly-modest annual return in comparison with other possible investments that could appreciate in value. However, the return generally accumulates tax-free, and might even be tax-free at the time of sale. That tax-free gain is good for building wealth.

One basic problem is that there are costs associated with obtaining the appreciation, and these costs can be substantial. For starters, there are usually significant state and local property taxes, which is one of only a few places where the government directly taxes wealth not income. *Payouts* for property taxes can *eat significantly* into the otherwise tax-deferred or perhaps tax-free appreciation.

Another major cost is for repairs, upkeep and perhaps continuing upgrades. Plumbing and heating systems can fail. A new kitchen might easily end up costing more than it adds to the value of the house. To the extent that this happens, the kitchen becomes a depreciating not appreciating asset. Not everything one might do to upgrade a house will increase the value of the house by at least an equivalent amount—most upgrades return only a fraction of their initial cost in resale. As an investment, the homeowner needs to be very careful here, and tread carefully. You can become poor (not wealthy) making upgrades. The neighborhood matters too, and you do not want to over-improve a house beyond what is considered normal for the neighborhood.

Perhaps an even more important problem in the use of residential real estate as an appreciating asset is that residential real-estate markets are always very local, and local markets frequently do not follow national, regional or even statewide trends in terms of appreciation (or depreciation). To build wealth using residential real estate, one needs to be constantly aware not only with respect to what is happening nationally, but also of local trends and markets, even trends going on within your subdivision and street. This involves studying the details of what is happening within the local economy.

> 1. *Is the local economy expanding or contracting?* Are there net population inflows or outflows?

> 2. *Will whatever you identify is happening with respect to economic and population growth likely be sustainable over a 5- or 10-year period, or is this a boom-and-bust economy?* If people leave the area will you be stuck with a house you cannot sell?
>
> 3. *What has happened to residential real estate values historically in your neighborhood over, say, the past 10 years?* Have the values been stable, or gone up or down significantly?
>
> 4. *What do you observe on the horizon that could make people want to either move into or out of the community in large numbers?*

Real estate agents often say "Location! Location! Location!" They observe not only what is happening within the local economy overall, but what is happening subdivision-by-subdivision and even street-by-street. Pricing trends for an entire city mask something way more complex. People not only want to live broadly within an area, but they are also particular about where they live within the area. This goes down to the subdivision and even street level. Bluntly put, some subdivisions and streets are sought after: others not so much, and some are even places to try and avoid. As a potential home-buyer, you need to be aware of all of this.

From an appreciation perspective, an aggressive pursuit-of-wealth strategy would be to attempt to identify houses located on streets and in subdivisions and locales that have not yet been identified by most buyers as being good places to locate, with the idea that in some not-too-distant future the area will be seen as highly desirable and be the place people want to live. This strategy potentially can lead to significant wealth creation if one calls this correct. But there is a downside to this strategy too, with a real possibility that one ends up owning real estate on a street where home values continue to decline over the longer term. The strategy is aggressive, but not risk-free.

A related concern in a growing area with population inflows is how difficult or easy it would be for builders to add to the housing stock by simply expanding subdivisions into adjoining unpopulated rural areas. Is the town or city adjoined by corn fields that could readily be converted into city lots, or are there real limits to such expansion?

For many decades, prices in many California real-estate markets were driven largely by strong local economies accompanied by population inflows as a result of expanding new high-paying jobs. Combine this with severe restrictions on builders with respect to the expansion of subdivisions, and you set up a situation where existing real estate is going to quickly become very pricey.

Note that the major cities in neighboring Arizona such as Phoenix ended up in a different place entirely price- and appreciation-wise. For example, the Phoenix area has also experienced major population inflows over the decades, but home prices have risen by much more modest levels. The key here is that builders in Arizona were usually able to respond to the population inflows by merely adding more lots and houses into the surrounding desert. As a wealth-creation strategy, the Phoenix house was usually at best, merely ok, but no get rich quick strategy.

California real estate prices in many areas have plummeted in recent years, despite the fact that the stock of homes has not increased significantly. This is now about employers seeing that the cost of doing business in California has become too pricey, and then moving elsewhere. Toyota recently started moving its main US headquarters from Southern California to Texas, for example, a location with much less expensive housing prices. The exception to all of this is the San Jose-Silicon Valley area, where homes remain very expensive given the interest in technology companies to operate in that particular location. I also need to note that high wages and salaries frequently tend to move the local real estate prices higher, particularly for the real estate considered to be located in a "prime" area relative to where the company paying the high-and-rapidly-rising salaries is located.

Farmland can be a good long-term investment, but even here values declined by more than 50 percent over only a few years in the early 1980s. Here are some average prices over time for an acre of farm real estate (technically, the value of land and buildings) in a number of states in the Midwest.

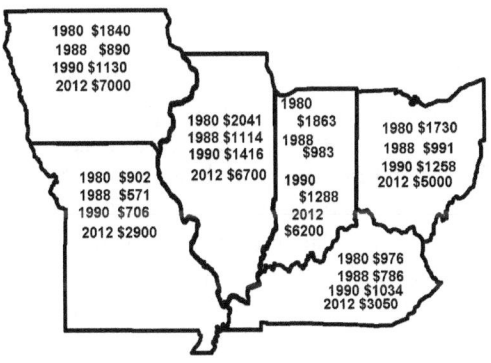

Using Iowa farm real estate as an example, the per-acre value was cut by over half between 1980 and 1988 ($1,840 in 1980: $890 by 1988), but then rebounded to $1,130 in 1990, just three years later.

How does the long-term appreciation in farm real estate values compare with residential housing? If I look at

Iowa farm real estate as an example for the 33-year time period 1980 through 2012, the end value of $7,000 per acre initially seems to be phenomenal. To determine the compound annual rate of return the equation $(\$7,000/\$1840)^{1/33}$ needs to be solved. This works out to a very modest annual rate of appreciation of 4.13 percent. Not a bad return, especially since the gains are not taxable as income until the farm real estate is sold, but nothing particularly outsized, either.

If I had been fortunate enough to make a purchase of Iowa real estate in 1988 rather than 1980, returns look substantially better for the 25-year period through 2012. In particular, the equation to be solved becomes $(\$7,000/\$890)^{1/25}$. This works out to a compound annual rate-of-return of 8.60 percent.. But once again, this would have required some luck to time the purchase, and, in particular, to buy farm real estate when others were getting out.

Wealth can be created by buying and holding farm real estate. Of course, what we are missing here is that farmland rented out to a farmer generates a stream of (taxable) rental income as well as the capital appreciation. Given the size of the investment, the rental income is not only taxable, but relative to the size of the investment, not particularly large. To illustrate, acre of Iowa farm real estate selling for $7,000 might be rented for $350-$400. This adds another 0.5 percent or so to the annual return.

As an investment, the big advantage is that taxes are not paid on any gains until the land is sold, and then at the marginal capital gains rate, not the rate for ordinary income. That the rental income taxable under ordinary federal and state income tax rates is small may be a plus not a minus for some investors.

Farmers can and do become wealthy by simply buying and then holding on to farm real estate, but they are not unique in this regard, and the value of the real estate can be at least as volatile year to year as non-farm residential real estate, if not more so. Other options for building wealth via tax-deferred capital gains may be better.

Chapter 6

Gold, Silver, Diamonds and Other Collectibles

Have you ever watched a commercial on TV for a company selling gold coins? Mostly, I just laugh. Invariably, the commercials attempt to create a world in which the economy is collapsing, the federal government is printing far too much paper money, and nearly everyone is out of work. We are on the verge of an apocalypse, economics-wise. Then the transition is made. The only way to deal with such an economic situation is to *own gold!*

What I find funniest about these ads is what *sounds like* solid economics to people interested in investing in gold has serious holes in it. Let us examine the errors in logic one at a time.

First, gold is a *precious metal*, meaning that most gold not in bars and coins is used in items such as jewelry. Jewelry is not a basic human necessity. It falls in the category of a *frill*, that is something which may be nice to own but certainly not a basic human necessity. Industrial uses of gold are very limited, especially compared to a less-precious metal such as silver. Mainly, a small amount of gold is used for making good electrical contacts, since gold does not tarnish or corrode. But there is no large industrial demand for gold.

A major component of gold demand comes from two sources—those interested in buying and holding gold coins, and from those interested in owning gold jewelry. Gold jewelry is a fashion item. I have talked to silver-haired women who tell me they do not like to wear gold jewelry because it clashes with their gray hair! The jewelry demand for gold is going to rise and fall with the fashion of the moment.

In India, gold jewelry is always considered to be the right gift for a bride. There is a cycle for weddings in India, with weddings occurring more frequently in some months than in others. This translates into a potential annual cycle in gold prices as well, driven in part by variation in world-wide demand for gold jewelry

Gold coins do not pay interest or otherwise generate any returns. Coins just sit there, perhaps appreciating in value under just the right (or, as the TV announcer claims, the *wrong*) set of economic conditions. But let us examine that reasoning more closely. The world is on the verge of economic collapse; the governments around the world have printed way too much paper money. The price of gold is soaring.

Well maybe not! The per-ounce price of gold is determined by the world-wide supply and demand for gold. If the economies around the world are quite bad, and people are bad-off, what makes you think that the same people who are struggling to meet basic needs will still have the money needed to bid up the price of gold to $2,500 an ounce? Maybe basic food items are in far greater demand. After all, you cannot *eat* gold coins or gold jewelry. How is it that you can somehow reasonably-conclude that gold prices will soar in the face of world-wide economic collapse?

If not gold, then maybe silver? An ounce of gold sells for 60 or 65 times the price of an ounce of silver. As a store of value, it will take a lot bigger safety-deposit box to store the same value of silver than gold. Silver is an *inconvenient* store of value.

However, unlike gold, silver has significant industrial uses. Silver is currently in strong demand for electronics parts in devices such as cell phones. At one time, a major industrial use for silver was as silver oxide in film. With digital photography, a major industrial use went away.

Silver coins, like gold coins, do not generate a stream of returns such as interest or dividend payments. The owner of silver coins just sits there, hoping that the price of the coins will appreciate. There is a silver demand for jewelry especially among the silver-haired ladies who want their jewelry to better match their hair color, but this is not a demand with significant growth prospects. With the fall-off in gold prices, TV commercials promote holding silver not gold, but the public does not seem to be buying into that, at least not to the point of significantly increasing the price of silver. Industrial uses notwithstanding, silver has experienced price volatility at least as violent as anything that has happened in gold.

If you want to speculate that the price of gold or silver will rise, the easy way to accomplish this is to buy and exchange-traded fund that invests in the gold bullion such as the fund traded as GLD on the equity markets. No premiums are paid to a TV marketer of coins, and no safety deposit box is needed to store the coins. There are also exchange-traded funds investing in silver, the largest being the one that trades under the ticker symbol SLV. It is not necessary to own either gold or silver coinage for delivery if one simply wants to speculate on the *possibility* of rising prices for the two metals.

What about diamonds? An ounce of gold is an ounce of gold, or nearly so. An ounce of silver is an ounce of silver. Exchange-traded funds investing in the metals are easily constructed, because of this.

Unlike gold and silver, no two diamonds are exactly alike. Diamonds ready for use in jewelry are graded on a scale involving the four "classic C" factors—that is, color, cut, clarity and carat weight. Grading a diamond is not a simple task, but requires professional skills. Further, two diamond graders might evaluate the same diamond and score it somewhat differently. And the grade determines the value.

An amateur might think that perfectly-clear diamonds would be the most valuable. But diamonds occasionally contain impurities that color them and make them even more valuable. For example a pink diamond or a gold-colored diamond might be very rare and valuable. Sometimes colorations add value, but sometimes colorations make the diamond less valuable.

Clarity has to do with the presence or absence of *inclusions* within the diamond. Often, these inclusions are tiny pieces of black non-diamond carbon like a tiny piece of embedded coal. No diamond is entirely free of inclusions, but in the highest-grade diamonds the inclusions are tougher to spot except under high magnification, and thus diamonds that look clear under all but the highest magnification are the most valuable, other C-factors being the same.

Diamond-cutting is a highly specialized skill, and some cutters have specialized skills that are essential in getting the most fire or brilliance out of the diamond. A good diamond cutter may also be able to cut the diamond in such a way that the inclusions in the raw diamond are less bothersome, if not eliminated entirely. So the value of the diamond as jewelry is at least partially based on the skill of the cutter who worked the raw stone.

Finally, there is the *carat weight* of the diamond, the characteristic most familiar to grooms purchasing engagement rings. Prices for diamonds broadly follow the weight of the diamond, other C-factors being equal. But, of course, other things are not equal. Anxious grooms, rich or not so rich, always have a specific budget for the engagement ring. Given a specific dollar amount in the budget, would she prefer a larger stone with many inclusions, or a smaller stone that has inclusions only visible under significant magnification? Would she prefer a larger stone with a less brilliant cut or a smaller stone with a more brilliant cut? These are no simple answers to these questions for sure, except to say that the largest carat-weight diamond that fits the budget is not necessarily the wisest choice.

Then there are the issues with the diamond trade. Historically, the raw diamond trade was largely a monopoly controlled by DeBeers Consolidated Mines from the mining to the cut stone ready to be set into a ring. The objective of DeBeers was to make sure that the supply of raw diamonds never outpaced the demand for diamonds, making certain that diamond prices steadily increased over time and never decreased.

Currently, the diamond trade is a bit more open, but the supply, and therefore the price of diamonds is still primarily controlled by only a few key players. The market is still by no means open like, say, the market for corn, soybeans or even gold and silver.

Then there are the jewelry stores—lots and lots of jewelry stores, stores that make a lot of their profits selling diamonds set in rings for anxious grooms to purchase. If this were not such a highly-profitable business, there would be far fewer jewelry stores, and jewelry stores would not be frequently located in high-rent shopping malls. The groom walking into such a store seeking a deal on a diamond for the bride already has one strike against him, and will almost certainly pay far more for the ring than the value of the graded-cut diamond and the precious metal setting. The only question is how much more. Fifty percent more? One-hundred percent? Three-hundred percent?

Given how the diamond market, diamonds do have an advantage over gold and silver in that prices tend to be less volatile over long periods of time. Generally, diamond prices increase over time. As an appreciating asset, however, there are still major issues in that most set diamonds are sold through jewelry stores at substantially above their real wholesale cost.

The only real question is at what point in time will the resale value of the diamond ring be equal to the original price paid to the jeweler? 10th anniversary? 20th anniversary? An anniversary still further out? By the time the divorce is finalized? Maybe this does not matter so long as the marriage hangs together. At least the diamond asset appreciated not depreciated over time. But as a financial investment, diamonds are not great.

There have been attempts to create exchange-traded funds that invest in raw diamonds, mimicking what is done with funds such as GLD and SLV. Because of the issues relating to the uniqueness of each diamond in terms of grade, along with the controlled nature of the diamond market itself, generally these have fallen flat. What has sometimes been referred to as the Diamonds ETF or DIA, is actually a stock index ETF investing instead in the Dow Jones Industrial Average index.

What about other collectibles as appreciating assets for financial investments? There are a wide range of collectibles that might increase in value over time, ranging from baseball cards and other sports memorabilia, to artwork, antique furniture, and even what I like to call a range of klitzy collectables such as Beanie Babies®, Cabbage Patch Dolls®, and Hummel® figurines. Each collectable has a following, and the people in the following enjoy becoming expert in whatever it is they happen to collect. Here are some thoughts about collecting as a wealth-building strategy.

1. *Nearly anything sold as a "new" collectible is not a collectible or appreciating asset, but likely depreciates in value instead.* These pseudo collectibles include Beanie Babies®, Cabbage Patch Dolls®, Hummel® figurines, Thomas Kinkade® prints, as well as practically anything sold in a magazine ad by a company with the term "Mint" somewhere in its name. You may want to own some of these items for whatever reason, but do not expect these to be appreciating assets.

2. *Collectibles often fluctuate wildly in value based on the current interest (demand) for the item as well as the existing supply.* Often, the best collectibles with respect to appreciation potential are items initially produced in large numbers but that most people quickly tossed, say the so called cardboard "ice cream box" that contained a model John Deere® combine sold as a toy in the 1950s. The boxes were particularly fragile, and most were quickly thrown in the trash. Toy collectors know that the box the toy came in is often more

valuable than the toy itself, which survived in larger numbers.

3. *If you had bought the rare Beanie Baby® Peanut-the-Elephant at anywhere near its initial retail price, at one point you could have sold it for substantially more than that.* However, if Peanut was acquired at a collector's price after the run-up, chances are you lost money.

4. *Hummel® figurines seldom appreciate in value except possibly for some very early and thus extremely rare items.* If there is a ready supply, chances are you can buy pre-owned figurines cheaper than what the figurine sold for originally.

5. The public has long been fascinated with the PBS television show called Antiques Roadshow, and the audience is especially fascinated when someone brings in a modest-looking painting bought at a garage sale for $5 that turns out to be by a comparatively famous artist and might now be worth as much as $20,000. This is a bit like winning the lottery, with similar long odds.

6. *I am always fascinated by the fact that most people who learn that they bought something now valuable for very little money almost invariably want to sell it for cash as quickly as possible.* Were this not true, the History channel would not have the hit pawn show built around people bearing items they want to sell. Has not the thought ever occurred to these people that the same painting might be worth $40,000 twenty years from now? Of course, they would be taking on some risk because of the possible decline in interest in works by a particular artist along with a gradual decline in the

price of the painting. However, the *urge* to convert potentially-appreciating assets into cash to be used in buying assets that depreciate in value runs large. The $20,000 painting could fund a *new car*, something that would almost assuredly be *all but worthless* twenty years from now.

7. *It is possible to make money with collectibles, but one first needs to be willing to develop the necessary knowledge and skills for each particular market.* Most people do not take the time or have the energy to do this. Collectibles do not generate an ongoing stream of returns or income. You collect only when you convert the collectible to cash, and most often this cash then quickly ends up going into depreciating, not appreciating, assets.

Chapter 7

Coping with Uncertainty

The opening lecture of a basic farm management course usually makes the following points:

Farming involves two sets of variables:

1. *Variables under the control of the decision maker* (i.e. what to plant, how much fertilizer to apply, when to plant and harvest, etc.)

2. *Variables that affect outcomes, but are not under the control of the decision maker (i.e. amounts and timing of rainfall, sunshine, hail or not, etc.).* Outcomes are measures like crop yields, which dramatically affect how much money the farmer makes.

Farmers as a group are experts at complaining about variables they do not control but affect outcomes and about how little money they make. It is way too wet, too dry, too warm, to cold or any of countless other events that can go wrong and make them unhappy. In farm country, honing one's own skills in doing this becomes a high art. It is a constant source of pleasure to see if you can complain more effectively about how bad the situation you are in than your neighbor does.

I knew a farmer who complained "We thought we bought the best farm equipment (farm machinery) there was, but it broke down anyway!" This evolved into an entire philosophy of life. He steadily complained about practically everything there was. He never assumed responsibility for his own actions. What went wrong was always the fault of something outside his control (or sometimes because of someone else, such as the obvious misbehavior of a neighboring farmer).

What appear at the beginning to be the best decisions possible sometimes, maybe frequently, (looking back in hindsight,) go all wrong. That is part of life. The best attitude is to not let it all get under your skin, and for certain, not to give up. The wealthiest people are able to pull themselves up from the bad things that happen, and keep plugging along. Sheer *determination* is a key to success.

The second principle of farm management states that no matter what happens, the farmer must *accept responsibility* for his or her own actions, in particular, decisions that could have been better in retrospect if you, the farmer, had only known what was going to happen to the variables outside your control. For example, if the farmer had known what the weather was going to be like during the growing season, a different crop might have been planted.

Accepting the fact that you made what turned out to be in retrospect a *wrong decision* is critical. Try to learn from your past mistakes, but do not assume that sometime soon you will be able to control the variables that are not under your control.

So, the basic farm management steps are:

1. *Identify the decision* to be made,

2. *Identify the variables that affect the outcomes of this decision* both in and out of your control,

3. *Make the decision* assuming that this will result in the most positive outcome,

4. *Bear the consequences* of your decision, good or bad,

5. *If you made mistakes, use these as a basis for learning how to improve your decision making* the next time around.

These same *management principles* could be observed and applied to a variety of different situations and careers, not just to farming. Not unlike farmers, politicians are frequently *experts* at *blaming* whatever problems they face on someone or something outside their control. The politician complains that "I would really like to fix this problem, and the reason I can't is because of (select from one of the following)":

1. "The misguided policies of the person who previously was in this position and messed things up so badly not even a person with my brains and resourcefulness can solve the problem now."

2. "Some other branch of government does not agree with me on how to fix the problem, and try as I might I cannot budge them."

3. "Some other political leader does not agree with me and therefore will not go along with my otherwise very excellent plans for getting to a solution."

Notice how each of these is an attempt to *not accept* any *personal responsibility* when things go wrong, but rather *deflect* personal responsibility on someone or something else outside their control. Never is the possibility that the politician is *not smart enough* to identify a way to solve the problem approached, as that would put the politician's skills in a bad light, and perhaps result in a loss in the next election. Politicians as a group tend to be not only self-absorbed but also very confident in their ability to identify and make correct decisions.

This blame game goes on to an equal degree in both political parties. Politicians are even better than farmers at refusing to accept *personal responsibility* for a decision gone wrong while attempting to deflect outcomes that do not measure up on some other person, persons or thing.

Voters sometimes wake up and realize that politicians are elected and paid to solve problems, and even in the political world, placing blame elsewhere for not getting a problem solved will go only so far. Politicians who try to always put the blame for undesirable outcomes on anyone or anything that obstructs them soon become unpopular with voters, who will invariably seek to find an alternative leader who does not do this. But then a different politician is elected, and he or she quickly starts trying to protect him or herself by blaming anyone or anything but themselves, and the entire process repeats endlessly.

When things go bad, the game of placing the blame elsewhere begins. CEOs and other non-farm firm managers are not immune from the same disease, that is, constantly placing the blame for something not turning out right on others. CEOs have even a larger set of options in placing blame. A CEO might complain that retail sales were off because Easter came too late (or too early) this year. Maybe the weather suddenly turned too cold (or too hot) so people did not get out to buy. Or perhaps gasoline got too expensive and people stayed home. The list of excuses for nonperformance within a shareholder-owned company goes on and on, each being a rationale for why the company did not do well that places the blame on anyone or anything other than the quality of the decision making by company executives. Sometimes, shareholders believe the excuses, but often not, and then the shares get sold, and the stock price declines.

At the same time, when a company does well and makes more money than expected, executives like to claim that this was largely as a result of their own *superior decision-making skills*. The tables get turned, entirely.

Average people, that is, people who are not corporate executives, often muddle through life with this same messed-up thinking and playing a very similar blame game. Some people never want to admit that they cannot control variables outside of their control, and they go along finding someone or something else to blame whenever anything does not go the way they wanted it to.

Generally these people are unhappy, and often they are severely depressed. Things that went right are always overwhelmed by things that went wrong. The cup is always half-empty, not half-full.

There is a tendency for these people to not accept personal responsibility for any decision that did not turn out as hoped in a perfect world. Finding someone or something else to blame is a critical part of their psyche. These people normally find comfort only when they are really depressed over how events turned out. It is almost as if they *want* their decisions to turn out badly. This permits them to play on the sympathy of others.

This all becomes a game titled "I'll bet you my life is even more messed up than your life is!" They act as if they are somehow the only ones who have ever faced a problem, and that everyone else lives in a perfect world, or nearly so. These people tend to live only in the present, believing that tomorrow will never come for them, anyway. I am convinced that for these people this leads to spending lots of money on consumption today using the assumption that they will not be around for tomorrow anyway.

From the perspective for doing long-term financial planning, this is an unmitigated disaster, because every decision involving finance ends up being the decision that makes the person happy right now rather than improving their lot at some time in the future.

In turn, this leads not only to overspending, but also to high short-term debt (They can't collect the debt on my credit cards if I am dead, can they?). Furthermore, this leads to spending allocations that are almost totally directed toward rapidly-depreciating goods, not often appreciating goods that might take a while to increase in value.

The basic principles of farm management can be readily adapted to more general financial planning:

1. *In making longer-term investments in generally appreciating-assets, there are variables you control.* The obvious one is "what is the specific asset?", but there are others as well.

2. *There are also variables that are outside of those you control.* For example, in investing in a stock, you do not run the company day-by-day, nor can you control the course of the markets over time.

3. *Things will go often wrong, or at least turn out differently from what you expected or hoped for in an ideal world.*

4. *You* are personally responsible for the decisions you make regardless of what happens. Specifically, the blame games politicians, CEOs and others play are not allowed. This is normally not a comforting place for people who have attempted to live their lives trying to deflect blame to someone or something else. You knew that going in. In stock-market investing, these same people, if they get into the markets at all, tend to buy stocks when prices are soaring and sell when prices are cheap, exactly opposite from what they should be doing. This makes sense only if they believe the stock market is nothing but a roulette wheel anyway, and they get satisfaction (utility) by bragging to their friends and neighbors about how much money they were able to lose in the market as a sympathy play. Buying stocks for these people becomes no different from buying a lottery ticket as they secretly enjoy the sympathy associated with having lost at what they believe is a game stacked against them.

5. *Risk-taking, and along with that bearing responsibility for what happens, is a very important a part of investing in generally-appreciating assets.* Markets do not go up every day: Houses don't go up in value every day. Sometimes both fall hard, and you need to be prepared for this.

6. *I repeat, investing in generally-appreciating assets largely involves deferring current consumption with the expectations of future gains.* Generally, wealthy people live for a future with an improved financial position. Non-wealthy people believe that today is all that matters, so the only purchases that matter are those that make me happier right now. I wonder what would happen if everyone decided to eat a

$4 meal at a fast food joint instead of a $7 meal, and use the remaining $3 that was saved to invest in a stock (maybe not MCD!). Do this over and over again and one's waistline would benefit just as will one's generally-appreciating asset position. This idea seems surprisingly simple, but most people never think in those terms. That is why most people live from paycheck to paycheck, have all but no savings, high debt loads (and perhaps, big waistlines).

Chapter 8

Equity Investing: The Basics

Equity investing inherently involves:

1. *Decision making in the face of uncertainty with respect to what the future might hold,* and

2. *Being willing to deal with the consequences when outcomes are not what you expected or wanted.*

Specifically, how an investor deals with uncertainty, but specially how an investor copes with *unanticipated outcomes*, in large measure determines whether or not wealth increases over time.

For starters, let me suppose that an investor makes an investment of $10,000 and the investment over the course of the year drops in value by 35 percent, leaving the value of the investment one year later at only $6,500. Three responses are possible:

1. *Sell out taking the $3500 loss and vowing never to make another investment like that.* (This outcome certainly *proves* that the individual should have just *spent* the money buying a depreciating asset instead, and that investing is "for the birds.")

2. *Hang tight, and expect the investment will eventually recover the losses and more.* (Things are never quite as bad as they appear to be).

3. *Use the decline in the value of the asset to buy some more at the lower price.*

Most beginning investors think that the choice of the particular investment to be made is mostly what determines outcomes. However, wise investors realize that a fundamental rule is that *timing* of the investment may matter as much or more than *what* the investment is. It is not so much about *what* you bought as it is about *when* you bought it and at *what price* you got in.

So far as equity investing goes, there is no simpler investment than an S&P 500 index fund, a fund that mimics the performance of Standard and Poor's index of mostly large- and medium-cap US companies. Perhaps the most famous of all index funds is the one sold by Vanguard under the symbol VFINX. That is the fund Warren Buffett was talking about using for his wife in his estate. Buffett is attracted to the Vanguard fund because expenses are very low, so it closely follows the index plus the dividends the companies in the index pay.

Here is how the S&P 500 index fund (VFINX) performed over the 6 years by placing a $10,000 investment in the fund at the start of 2008 to the end of 2013.

Year	VFINX	$10,000
2008	-37.02%	$6,298
2009	26.49%	$7,966
2010	14.91%	$9,154
2011	1.97%	$9,334
2012	15.82%	$10,811
2013	32.18%	$14,290

The year 2008 was a year of massive losses in the stock market. The S&P 500 index fund VFINX lost more than 35 percent that year, exactly a 37.02 percent loss. This means that at the end of 2008, the original investment would be worth only $6,298. And the stock market was supposed to be a place to buy assets that broadly appreciate not depreciate!

How would *you* have dealt with such a massive one-year loss? This is a classic example of learning to deal with outcomes not being what you hoped, expected or wanted. Had you spent your money on a motor vehicle instead of the dumb stock-market index fund, surely the motor vehicle would not have depreciated by 37.02 percent in only one year. Maybe building wealth in the equities market is *not* for you and instead you should always spend money on depreciating assets instead, like motor vehicles. A loss like this is both the start and the end of investing for many who cannot cope with the undesired consequences of unexpected outcomes.

How about the strategy of just hanging tight after experiencing the 2008 loss of 37.02 percent? After all, had Mrs. Warren Buffett had owned her fund at the start of 2008, she would have experienced the same 37.02 percent loss. (Wealthy or not so wealthy, the same percentage loss would have applied.) This might still be a painful strategy.

After all, the market could have followed the 37.02 percent VFINX loss with another loss of over 25 percent. Sometimes in the equity markets, losses are followed by still more losses one year after another.

As it turned out, however, the 37.02 percent loss in 2008 was followed by a 26.49 percent *gain* in 2009. This sounds like a decent recovery, but be very careful with the numbers here. The original $10,000 investment is still worth only $7,966 at the end of 2009, with a loss of over 20 percent on the original investment.

How can that be? Well, even if a loss of 37.02 percent is followed by an equal percentage gain of 37.02 percent, that gain would still not put you close to the original investment value, because the gain is not calculated based on the original $10,000 invested, but rather the $6,298 value after the loss of 37.02 percent. A 37.02 percent percentage loss followed by the same percentage gain gets the value back to only $8,630, still nearly 14 percent under the original investment value.

The investor who simply hangs tight with the initial VFINX investment does not get the full amount of the initial investment back until late 2012, and 2012 ends with the investor being up by only $811 on the original $10,000. That is what I call a long wait for a small return, just over a total 8 percent in the space of 5 years. Perhaps this is slightly higher than a certificate of deposit would have paid at a bank, but not by much (1.57 percent compounded annually over 5 years). To have the courage, discipline and patience as well as the personality to accept such a paltry return for such an outcome is very rare indeed. This looks to be a fool's game.

By the end of 2013, things look a lot rosier, however. The $10,000 invested in VFINX at the start of 2008 is worth $14,290, for a cumulative return of 42.9 percent for the 6 years. This is a compound annual rate-of-return of $(\$14,290/\$10,000)^{1/6} = 6.13$ percent, far better than bank certificates of deposit were yielding over the same period. But, years of being underwater were suffered to get there.

So, what went wrong? Was VFINX simply the wrong investment for the time, or could simple changes have been made that would affect outcomes in a positive way?

Most financial planners correctly advise investor-clients that if they have a sum of money to invest that they should invest all of the funds right away, and not a little at-a-time. In most markets that are usually gradually rising over time, this is the correct advice. But it is not the correct advice if markets are in danger of falling back in a significant way. Specifically, the years 2008-2013 were years for client-investors to *not follow* the classic advice.

Suppose instead of investing the entire $10,000 at the start of 2008, the investor instead decided to invest the same $10,000, but only $2,000 each year from 2008 to 2012. Then by the start of 2013, the entire $10,000 would be invested. Small investors might like this strategy because they only have to come up with $2,000 to invest in any one year, not the entire $10,000. How would outcomes have changed? Here is a table showing what would have happened.

Year	VFINX	$2,000	Invested Funds
2008	-37.02%	$1,260	$2,000
2009	26.49%	$4,123	$4,000
2010	14.91%	$7,036	$6,000
2011	1.97%	$9,214	$8,000
2012	15.82%	$12,988	$10,000
2013	32.18%	$17,168	$10,000

The initial $2000 investment is worth only $1,260 at the end of 2008, for the same 37.02 percent loss. But since the investor only had $2,000 not $10,000 invested, the dollar loss is much smaller at the end of 2008 than it was in the first illustration.

Further, in most years there is less money at risk. Even more importantly, by the end of 2009, the investor has $4,000 in the market, but the value of the fund at the end of the year is above water at $4,123. Further, the investor is above water in each of the remaining years as well, with the fund being worth more than the accumulated amount invested in each year. By the end of 2013, the fund is worth a whopping $17,168, far better than the $14,290 with all the money invested at the start of 2008.

This is a far more conservative investment strategy than putting all the investment dollars in the market at the beginning of the period. It yields greater returns in part because of the way returns evolved from the start of 2008 through the end of 2013. Who would have expected such massive equity losses in 2008? For that matter, who would have expected so many years of steady gains for the S&P 500 in the years that followed? One thing you quickly learn in investing is that practically anything can happen from one year to the next.

The decreases in stock prices in 2008 were in large measure because scared investors were falling over each other to exit the market when prices started to decline. Investors hate to lose money, and the consequence of that is that the stock markets are frequently more volatile than they would otherwise be. Stock prices increased again as soon as investors regained some confidence about what the future could hold.

I could now go into fancy macroeconomic logic which claims that most of the gains in the stock market since 2008 has been due to the fact that the Federal Reserve has been printing money as fast as they can, keeping interest rates low and inflating stock prices beyond where they realistically should be. The gold bugs make that argument, too. If one believes that argument, then perhaps the market is due for another significant selloff with perhaps a 25 percent decline in VFINX. But if we all believe that, then we should all be holding cash that we will be ready to invest as soon as prices get lower.

Suppose, however, that an investor concluded that equities were expensive at the start of 2008, and delays investing the $10,000 to the start of 2009, after VFINX has dropped 37.02 percent. Here are the results.

Year	VFINX		invested funds
2008	-37.02%	$0	0
2009	26.49%	$12,649	$10,000
2010	14.91%	$14,535	$10,000
2011	1.97%	$14,821	$10,000
2012	15.82%	$17,166	$10,000
2013	32.18%	$22,690	$10,000

Given how 2008 to 2013 actually evolved, this was the correct strategy. The investor more than doubled the $10,000 to $22,690 by the end of 2013, by taking advantage of the cheap equity prices at the start of 2009. This is also the strategy that requires the most *courage*. In this case, the there were two critical judgment calls on the part of the investor.

The first call was that stocks had gotten too pricey at the start of 2008 given the weak economic outlook. The second was that after the 37.02 percent selloff, stocks really were historically cheap and that a subsequent double-digit loss year was not going to follow in 2009. Making either of these calls correctly and implementing them involves some dumb luck as well as courage.

Making this work also requires the investor to do some things that are much the opposite of what other investors are doing. This is a classic example of the big payoffs involved when you buy equities exactly when everyone else around you is selling. This is what *courage* and *discipline* in building wealth is really all about. It is also all about more than doubling your investment dollars in a total of 6 years using only the simplest of equity funds. You cannot do that well at the local bank for sure.

And what if the investor had made the wrong judgment call at the start of 2008, and that instead of stocks going down in price, they continued to rise in all of 2008? The same investor then perhaps would have been better off investing the entire $10,000 at the start of 2008, and then just let it ride.

To conclude, getting the timing of purchases right frequently matters a lot more than what the specific investment is, and many investors fret a lot about what they are investing in as opposed to focusing their attention on making purchases at a good price. The catch is that if you sit and wait for still cheaper prices without investing, the market could go off without you!

Chapter 9

Equity Investing: Actively-Managed Funds

Investing in a simple S&P 500 index fund is an easy way to get involved in equity investing, and is possible to still do very well without getting involved in anything more complicated. However, I am not a big fan of index-fund investing and, in particular, I am not fond of index funds that primarily invest in large-cap stocks.

The S&P 500 index is what is called a *market capitalization-weighted* stock index. That means that companies with large market capitalizations (total shares times the price of each share) make up a greater share of the index than do smaller market-capitalization companies. As a direct consequence of the market-cap weighting, the S&P 500 index on any given day is nearly 90 percent driven by prices of large-cap stocks and only a little over 10 percent driven by prices of smaller companies in the index. Further, a company has to be at least a certain size before it is even considered for inclusion in the S&P 500 index. Large-cap companies, having already achieved large sizes and market capitalizations, are often slower-growing than firms considered to be mid or small-cap. This can drag down returns over time.

Of course, it is possible to purchase funds that mimic the performance of other indices such as mid or small market cap indices. Of course, the smaller the company, the greater the chance of bankruptcy, so small- and mid-cap indexes can be more volatile than large cap indexes.

Then there is the issue of value versus growth. An average stock price-to-earnings ratio (P/E ratio, for short) for the companies in the S&P 500 might be, say, 15. Growth stocks are those for companies that have a higher P/E ratio than the average: value stocks typically have a P/E of less than the average for the entire group. Investors are willing to pay a higher price per share for growth stocks for the same earnings than for value stocks largely because they believe that the average growth-stock company will be an above-average grower of earnings going forward.

Value stocks often are the stocks of companies that may have steady earnings, but these companies could be stodgy in terms of the rate of growth over time. When the market is doing well, growth stocks tend to do extraordinarily well. When the market is struggling and perhaps declining, value stocks frequently hold their values better than growth stocks do, as they already are selling at relatively low P/E ratios.

To me, the stock market *sweet spot* is in the sub-group of stocks that are classified as *mid-cap value*, If Warren Buffett really wants to buy an index fund to back an annuity for his wife, I would advise him out of an S&P 500 index fund such as VFINX, and instead go into a mid-cap value index fund such as Vanguard's mid-cap value fund that trades under the symbol VMVIX. The downside risk would be less, and the upside potential would be greater, given the mid-cap rather than large-cap market capitalization of the companies in the VMVIX index. Here are the data for VMVIX using a simple one-time $10,000 investment.

Equity Investing: Actively-Managed Funds

Year	VMVIX	$10,000
2008	-36.64%	$6,336
2009	37.61%	$8,719
2010	21.63%	$10,605
2011	-0.44%	$10,558
2012	15.91%	$12,238
2013	37.42%	$16,818

VMVIX loses nearly as much as VFINX in 2008, but the recovery in 2009 is much stronger. Better still, the original $10,000 investment is above water by 2010, not 2012 as it was for the S&P 500 index fund. Finally, the end-of-2013 value for VMVIX is $16,818 versus $14,290 for VFINX, the S&P 500 index fund, a $2,527 difference just for being in the *right* rather than the *wrong* index fund! To me, the extra money to be made by going with mid-cap value index fund instead of the S&P 500 index fund is some of the lowest-hanging fruit in the investment world.

But, should you just go with an index fund or instead seek out an *actively-managed* fund? An index fund is passive in that there is no active stock picking beyond any changes needed to make sure the fund mimics its particular index. As a consequence, expenses are very low. Advocates for index-fund investing point out that the low expenses are a key reason to buy index funds rather than actively-managed funds.

With an actively-managed fund, there is active picking of stocks that are included in the fund, as well as active buying and selling. This can lead not only to higher expenses but also higher income taxes for the investor, as realized appreciation in stocks not offset by the sale of stocks that lost value become realized capital gains for the fund shareholder (even though the shareholder did not sell the fund itself).

So is it all worth it? It is true that, on average, actively-managed funds probably do not outperform their respective indexes. However, contrary to what some investors believe, it is not particularly difficult to find actively-managed funds that beat an S&P 500 index fund over the longer haul. The trickier part is whether these actively-managed funds can beat the particular style box index fund (specific market cap, small, medium or large; value, growth or both) that is most similar to where the actively-managed fund is positioned. Of course, some fund managers are free to roam anywhere they think returns will be greater and include both growth and value stocks at a wide range of market capitalizations, small, mid and large.

A long-time favorite fund of mine is Fidelity Low-Priced (FLPSX), managed since its inception in 1986 by Joel Tillinghast. Tillinghast is highly regarded within the mutual-fund industry as being among the very best at what he does, managing a huge fund mostly containing a very large number of mid-cap companies. He has a long track record of regularly outperforming the S&P 500 index fund, if not in absolutely every year.

Historically, the fund invested mostly in mid-cap value companies that could be purchased cheaply (under $25 a share) and at low P/E ratios. In the last decade or so the fund increasingly invests in slightly higher- P/E and higher-priced mid-cap stocks, which by Fidelity's definition made it more nearly a mid cap *blend* as opposed to an actively-managed mid-cap *value* fund. But the real question still is whether or not, in doing this, it can beat the performance of Vanguard's mid-cap value index fund VMVIX. Here are the data for FLPSX.

Year	FLPSX	$10,000
2008	-36.17%	$6,383
2009	39.08%	$8,877
2010	20.70%	$10,715
2011	-0.06%	$10,709
2012	18.50%	$12,690
2013	34.31%	$17,044

FLPSX handily outstripped the S&P 500 index fund with an end value of $17,044 versus $14,290 for VFINX. FLPSX beat the mid-cap value index fund as well, but by a much smaller amount, $17044 versus $16818 for VMVIX.

Since FLPSX also invests in mid-cap growth stocks, it might be useful to also compare the data with the data for Vanguard's mid-cap growth index fund that trades under the symbol VMGIX. Here are the data for that fund.

Year	VMGIX	$10,000
2008	-47.07%	$5,293
2009	42.54%	$7,545
2010	28.93%	$9,727
2011	3.84%	$10,101
2012	15.81%	$11,698
2013	32.02%	$15,443

As I expected, the mid-cap growth companies lost more in the down market of 2008 than the mid-cap value companies did, but then had a larger percentage gain in 2009. In 2008 this index fund had a whopping loss of 47.07 percent, all but halving the initial investment. VMVIX was above water by the end of 2010, but it took

VMGIX to the end of 2011 to get there. Most importantly, the end value was $15,443. This beats the $14,290 of VFINX but is way below the $16,818 of the value index fund VMVIX.

And Fidelity would be happy to know that Tillinghast's actively-managed fund FLPSX beats the mid-cap growth index fund FMGIX by a far wider margin than it beat FMVIX on the value side.

At Fidelity, long-time fund manager William Danoff is nearly as famous as Joel Tillinghast. Danoff's flagship fund, Fidelity Contrafund (FCNTX), which he has managed since 1990, focuses on owning large-cap stocks on the growth rather than value side of the spectrum. Thus, the S&P 500 index fund VFINX is a more-nearly valid benchmark than the performance of the mid-cap index funds.

Since 2008 through 2013, the numbers for VFINX were

Year	VFINX	$10,000
2008	-37.02%	$6,298
2009	26.49%	$7,966
2010	14.91%	$9,154
2011	1.97%	$9,334
2012	15.82%	$10,811
2013	32.18%	$14,290

The comparable numbers for FCNTX are

Year	FCNTX	$10,000
2008	-37.16%	$6,284
2009	29.23%	$8,121
2010	16.93%	$9,496
2011	-0.14%	$9,482
2012	16.26%	$11,024
2013	34.15%	$14,789

What strikes me as being important about these numbers is how close they are to the numbers for the S&P 500 index fund, thus supporting my thesis that large-cap managers have a great deal of difficulty in beating the overall market. Danoff almost exactly matched the S&P 500 losses in 2008, then came back a bit stronger than VFINX in 2009. The risk/volatility profile of FCNTX is approximately equal to VFINX. The 2013 end value for Danoff's fund is $14,789 versus 14,290 for VFINX, a $499 difference in favor of the actively-managed fund over the 6 years.

To conclude. If one wants to invest in mutual funds that mimic market indices, be careful in choosing the index that you are mimicking. I continue to believe that over the long haul, the mid-caps are usually the place most investors should to be, and that the value side helps limit downside risk in market selloffs. So, if I were advising Warren Buffett, I would tell him that he really needs to focus on mid-cap value indices for his wife's fund, not the S&P 500.

There is also some support here for going with a good actively-managed fund, not following what Vanguard advocates that active managers cannot ordinarily beat the indexes over the long haul. I have never been enthusiastic about actively-managed large-cap funds. There are a relatively small number of large-cap companies, and most of them are in the S&P 500 index fund. An active manager of a large-cap fund can do some picking-and-choosing, emphasizing some companies and largely ignoring others, but in the end, the fund's holdings usually end up being not that much different from the S&P 500 index. Given the expenses of active management, manager fees and the costs associated with stock trading, it is often tough for a large-cap fund to outperform a simple S&P 500 index fund. Buffett is right about that.

If an actively-managed fund is focusing on mid- and small-caps, the actively-managed fund can usually distinguish itself at least somewhat from the index funds for the particular overall market capitalization, small- or mid-cap. This sets up preconditions necessary for an actively-managed fund to outperform its index, which the best-run actively-managed funds can do on a consistent long-term basis.

Chapter 10

Equity Investing: Sector Funds

Most equity funds invest in stocks encompassing a wide variety of sectors within the economy. Investing in different sectors is one way of mitigating risk, but especially so if the sectors tend not to move together over time. Also, there are particular sectors that will likely hold up relatively well when the rest of the economy is doing poorly. Generally, when an economy is declining, some sectors will do relatively better than others.

For example, in a recession people will still have to eat, buy groceries, and get health care services if they are sick. Expenditures on *consumer staples* usually hold up better in a weak economy than do expenditures on *consumer discretionary* items. Examples of a consumer discretionary items would be the purchase of a new car or perhaps furniture for the house. In a weak economy, some expenditures can readily be deferred. For example, in a recession, sales of new cars might decline, but sales of used cars and parts or repairs for vehicles might increase. Consumers might easily defer buying a new sofa for the den or living room in a weak economy.

In the stock market, there are three kinds of risk:

1. *Market risk*. When the stock market falls, a lot of different share prices tend to fall together. When the market rises, a lot of share prices increase

together. Market risk normally arises because of significant national and international events that either affect the market positively or negatively, including political events, new economic information, even wars.

2. *Sector-risk*. Sometimes events affect one sector of the economy more than others. All companies within a specific sector might either rise or fall in tandem, depending on whether the event is a positive or a negative for companies within a sector. A report from Microsoft that sales of Windows software is down might result in Hewlett Packard (HPQ) shares to also fall, since HPQ sells a lot of laptop computers that use Windows. Even though HPQ has not yet reported weak sales, weak sales of Windows might signal investors to also avoid HPQ stock, as their laptop sales might be down too.

3. *Company-specific risk*. Company managers might do either really smart or really dumb things. Smart things cause company profits to rise: dumb things cause company profits to fall, and share prices normally move with company profits. Not every company or manager in a sector is equally brilliant or stupid. The smart managers are rewarded with an increase in the price of the company stock. Dumb managers get to watch as the stock price falls.

In purchasing a sector-specific mutual fund, you are still subject to market risk and sector risk, but the fund manager is presumably attempting to avoid company-specific risk by picking and choosing from the companies within a sector.

Fidelity Investments sells over 40 sector-specific funds covering all parts of the economy. There are technology funds, health care funds, financial funds, funds that invest in consumer staples, industrial equipment, transportation, housing, and so on. It is up to the investor to choose the sectors with the most promising outlooks in terms of share price.

Attempting to keep current on what is happening in forty-plus sectors and sector funds poses a considerable challenge. Instead, over the past two decades, I have focused on a comparatively small subset of sectors. Four sectors I have watched for a long time are consumer staples (FDFAX), health care (FSPHX), electronics (FSELX) and energy services (FSESX). I used to also look at banking (FSRBX) a lot, but that sector has interested me less since the banking crisis that began in 2007.

Another interesting sector fund is the gold and precious metals fund (FSAGX). That fund invests partly in gold bullion, and partly in gold mining stocks, as well as in companies that mine silver, diamonds and similar. If one wants to place a bet on rising gold prices, the fund could beat owning the coins or bars themselves.

Two of these funds I would rate as defensive, consumer staples (FDFAX) and health care (FSPHX). In a deteriorating economy, both should hold up better than an index fund representing the entire S&P 500.

In contrast, both electronics (FSELX) and energy services (FSESX) might do worse than the S&P 500 when the S&P 500 is falling. However, FSELX does particularly well when companies are expanding their businesses, as they are investing in new electronics technologies, computers using the latest chips and the like.

The performance of energy-services companies (FSESX) should be linked to the price of oil, given that drilling activity and the need for the equipment energy-services companies make rises (and falls) with the price of oil. Rising oil prices are also linked to a rapidly-growing economy.

Let me begin by making some simple comparisons between the benchmark S&P 500 index fund (VFINX), and these four sector funds. Once again, here is the data for VFINX and for health care (FSPHX).

Year	VFINX	$10,000
2008	-37.02%	$6,298
2009	26.49%	$7,966
2010	14.91%	$9,154
2011	1.97%	$9,334
2012	15.82%	$10,811
2013	32.18%	$14,290

Year	FSPHX	$10,000
2008	-32.44%	$6,756
2009	32.11%	$8,925
2010	16.96%	$10,439
2011	7.82%	$11,255
2012	21.39%	$13,663
2013	56.27%	$21,351

The health care sector fund lost less than the S&P 500 index fund in 2008, although not a lot less. More importantly, it outgained the S&P 500 fund in all subsequent years except for 2011, resulting in a nice gain over the 6-year period, more than doubling the initial $10,000 investment to $21,351 in the 6 years through the end of 2013. People tend to spend a little less on health care in a weak economy, but health care spending rebounds as the economy strengthens.

The consumer staples fund (FDFAX) data are

Year	FDFAX	$10,000
2008	-22.30%	$7,770
2009	20.94%	$9,397
2010	15.20%	$10,825
2011	8.84%	$11,782
2012	15.39%	$13,596
2013	21.63%	$16,536

The 22.3 percent loss for FDFAX was in 2008 was far smaller than the loss for the S&P 500 index fund, and the fund posted a nice gain in every subsequent year. This is the fund for those that spend sleepless nights worrying about losses. The end of 2013 value of 16,536 was less than what the health-care fund gained, but still beat the S&P 500 index fund by a substantial margin.

The electronics (FSELX) data are

Year	FSELX	$10,000
2008	-49.87%	$5,013
2009	84.99%	$9,274
2010	16.84%	$10,835
2011	-8.49%	$9,915
2012	3.60%	$10,272
2013	39.18%	$14,297

The fund lost nearly 50 percent in 2008, but then recovered with a whopping 85 percent gain in 2009. Subsequent years have been everywhere. To get the almost the exact same end-of-2013 value as VFINX, the investor has to deal with much more year-after-year volatility.

The data for the energy services fund (FSESX) are

Year	FSESX	$10,000
2008	-63.16%	$3,684
2009	61.96%	$5,967
2010	27.92%	$7,632
2011	12.56%	$8,591
2012	2.57%	$8,812
2013	27.58%	$11,242

In 2008, the price of crude oil halved in value (or worse). A decline in the price of crude by a specific percentage will result in a much larger percentage decline in the profits of energy-service companies, as drillers drastically cut back on new drilling until the crude price recovers. Subsequent years showed gains for FSESX as the crude oil price moved back up, but the gains were all over the place year to year. The end of 2013 value is $11,242, only a little more than the initial $10,000, and in five of the six years the investor was underwater.

There are other possible strategies. Instead of investing $10,000 in only one fund, what about investing only $2,500 in each of the four funds at the start of 2008? The resulting numbers are

Year	4-sector combination
2008	$5,806
2009	$8,391
2010	$9,933
2011	$10,386
2012	$11,586
2013	$15,857

That diversification strategy beats the S&P 500 index fund (VFINX) in every year but 2008.

Yet another strategy might be to simply go with the two defensive sectors consumer staples (FDFAX) and health care (FSPHX), and splitting the $10,000 investment by putting $5,000 in each at the beginning of 2008. The numbers result in a nice $18,983 value in the end of 2013 from the $10,000 initially invested. This is a simple investment strategy that yields quite impressive results, with only modest volatility.

Year	two defensive sectors
2008	$7,213
2009	$9,246
2010	$10,649
2011	$11,510
2012	$13,633
2013	$18,983

I have been complaining that the entire financial sector has not been a great sector for investors over the past half-dozen years. Do the numbers back that conclusion? The answer is, yes. Here are the same numbers for Fidelity's banking sector fund (FSRBX).

Year	FSRBX	$10,000
2008	-37.48%	$6,252
2009	5.05%	$6,568
2010	21.44%	$7,976
2011	-13.31%	$6,914
2012	22.42%	$8,464
2013	39.38%	$11,798

The banking fund (FSRBX) experienced a 37.48 percent loss in 2008, which seems not that bad in comparison with the S&P 500 index fund (VFINX) which was down 37.02 percent in 2008, but this was after a 21.18 percent loss for FSRBX in 2007. In 2007, VFINX was *up* 5.39 percent. The 2013 end value was $11,798, but FSRBX was underwater (below the $10,000 initial investment) for all of the previous 5 years. I think I have been wise to avoid this sector entirely.

The 2013 end value for FSRBX of $11,798 may look superior to the $11,242 end value for energy services (FSESX). FSESX was underwater in all but 2013 too, but at least it was a steady climb upward from 2009. Here are the FSESX data one more time.

Year	FSESX	$10,000
2008	-63.16%	$3,684
2009	61.96%	$5,967
2010	27.92%	$7,632
2011	12.56%	$8,591
2012	2.57%	$8,812
2013	27.58%	$11,242

In 2007, FSRBX *lost* 21.18 percent. In 2007, FSESX *gained* 55.21 percent. So the FSESX loss of 63.16 percent was a *one-time occurrence* coming immediately after a gain of 55.21 percent. Remember, in 2008 the price of crude oil dropped by over 50 percent.

As an investor in FSESX, you might have taken two possible positions on all of this. One possibility was that the big drop in crude prices was a *temporary occurrence* brought on largely by the really-nasty US and worldwide economic conditions. The second possibility was that the bad economic conditions that led to the low oil prices were going to continue for an indefinite period of time, and that crude oil prices might rebound a bit but certainly not double again in any reasonable time (i.e. 5-year) frame.

Which of these two views you held determined your investment strategy in response to seeing the 63.16 percent loss for FSESX at the end of 2008. If oil prices are going to come back in a significant way in the next five years, the proper response at the end of 2008 was to see a big sale going on in the stocks comprising FSESX and then to load up on the fund, starting at the very end of 2008.

If crude oil prices were going to continue to flounder over the next 5 years, the proper investment response was to sit on the sidelines watching others continue to lose money holding FSESX.

We know now what happened: oil prices quickly rebounded, and those that bought into FSESX at the *deeply discounted* FSESX price at the end of 2008 and then just hung on made a boatload of money. How much money? Let us look at the data from a $10,000 investment in FSESX *at the very end* of 2008, *after* the big drop.

Year	FSESX	$10,000
2008	-63.16%	$0
2009	61.96%	$16,196
2010	27.92%	$20,718
2011	12.56%	$23,320
2012	2.57%	$23,919
2013	27.58%	$30,516

A shrewd (and perhaps lucky) investor more than *tripled* the initial $10,000 investment simply by shifting the purchase from the start of 2008 to the end of 2008. This seems like a simple move, but it is loaded with psychological issues. Would *you* have the *courage* to dive in with $10,000 investment dollars after you had just seen the fund shares decline by 63.16 percent? Would you *worry* that such a huge loss could be followed by another big percentage decline (like FRBX did in both 2007 and 2008). Would you be worried that the economy (and with it, crude oil prices which are ultimately driving the FSESX price) might *never* recover, at least not in the foreseeable future.

In short, can you still sleep at night doing something like this, buying in right after what appears to be a big loss? Maybe you would have been better off using at least some of the money you could have invested to fund a big trip to Disney World® instead. Maybe buying the *assets that could appreciate, but not always* is for the birds!

Those who build wealth often have *courage* the rest of us might lack, along with the *discipline* to stick with an idea, even though it might not seem to be right in the short run. I have also noticed that the wealthy almost always save back some cash, waiting for opportunities to buy potentially-appreciating assets at times when prices seem unreasonably low. This is part of the money-management *discipline* that the non-wealthy frequently lack.

It is not only having the stomach for and the ability to sleep at night even after pursuing a potential opportunity like this, it is about managing one's cash assets well enough so that there is some cash still available when the real investment opportunities present themselves. If you have siphoned off all your available cash to buy a new SUV or to use on expensive vacations, you are never going to be in an asset position strong enough to take advantage of the really interesting investment opportunities that have the potential to build serious wealth when they present themselves.

What about employing this strategy with a precious metal fund, FSAGX? Would a similar strategy have worked there? The basic data on FSAGX show

Year	FSAGX	$10,000
2008	-20.49%	$7,951
2009	38.00%	$10,972
2010	35.25%	$14,840
2011	-16.34%	$12,415
2012	-12.43%	$10,872
2013	-51.41%	$5,283

An investor could have delayed purchase of the fund until the end of 2008, and then invested the entire $10,000. The results are

Year	FSAGX2	$10,000
2008	-20.49%	$0
2009	38.00%	$13,800
2010	35.25%	$18,665
2011	-16.34%	$15,615
2012	-12.43%	$13,674
2013	-51.41%	$6,644

This strategy temporarily looks quite good, in fact better than most of our other strategies, but only through 2011. Then, gold prices start to plummet, and with that, the value of shares of FSAGX. By the end of 2013 the delayed $10,000 investment is worth only $6,644. I do not like this strategy and fund at all.

Diversification of investable funds into different and completely-unrelated sectors is often good in terms of mitigating losses and making more consistent gains, but there is no point in diversifying into a sector that one believes has little promise. You are constructing a portfolio that best reflects you and your outlook, not trying to create a market index nor an index fund.

A basic problem I have with an S&P 500 index fund is that it has become far too heavily weighted into the finance and banking sectors, sectors that I do not like at all right now. An active manager of a diversified fund seeing this the same way I do can underweight sectors that the manager feels are not making progress. Stocks of a lot of big banks appear to be cheap, but they are cheap for god reasons.

Banks make less money in a low interest-rate environment. A bet on one of these cheap banking stocks is a bet that interest rates and bank profits will soon be heading strongly upward. I could be wrong, but I just do not see that happening any time soon. And it is my money that I am investing, so I get to decide.

I can still readily construct a diversified portfolio using sector funds that avoid sectors I particularly do not like. I like consumer staples, health care, technology and energy. Why not work within those four areas? One can readily do this using sector funds, as we have just shown. Or for a different approach, buy individual stocks, which is the topic for the next chapter.

Chapter 11

Equity Investing: Individual Stocks

Harry Markowitz co-won the Nobel memorial prize in economics in 1990 for his portfolio theory that forms the basis for the modern mutual fund industry. A basic Markowitz portfolio model would first identify four different stocks, stocks in four largely-unrelated sectors, sectors that usually do not move together, but each with good potential for making gains over the longer term. In making purchases of these four stocks in equal dollar amounts, a portfolio is constructed that mitigates downside risk while still having good potential for gains over the longer term.

I have already been applying some of the Markowitz theories in my four-sector mutual fund portfolio consisting of equal dollar amounts invested in four different sectors, consumer staples (FDFAX), health care (FSPHX), electronics (FSELX), and energy services (FSESX). These are four usually-unrelated sectors, and different variables affect the performance of each of these sectors.

A basic problem in the practical application of Markowitz portfolio theory is that in a market selloff, most stocks and sectors decline in tandem. However, they decline in varying degrees. The S&P 500 index fund declined by 37.02 percent in 2008. But two of the four sectors declined by less than that consumer staples (FDFAX, -22.3 percent) and health care (FPHSX, -32.44 percent). Two declined by more than VFINX, electronics (FSELX, -49.87 percent), and energy services (FSESX, -63.16 percent). How did the performance of the equal-weights portfolio ($2,500 invested in each of the four *unrelated* sectors) compare relative to the performance of the S&P 500 index fund VFINX? As it turns out, the four-sector fund beat VFINX in all years but 2008. That is not a surprising result given the really bad returns for both electronics and energy services in 2008. Here are the data. I am getting significantly more end-of-2013 gains with the four-sector portfolio, with year-to-year risk comparable to, if not a little better than, the S&P 500 index fund.

Year	VFINX	4 sector combination	difference
2008	$6,298	$5,806	-$492
2009	$7,966	$8,391	$424
2010	$9,154	$9,933	$779
2011	$9,334	$10,386	$1,052
2012	$10,811	$11,586	$775
2013	$14,290	$15,857	$1,566

The four-sector portfolio beat the S&P index fund in 5 of the 6 years, while in 5 of the 6 years incurring less risk than VFINX. By the end of 2013, the portfolio is up $1,566 over VFINX, a not insignificant sum.

It might be argued that the S&P 500 index fund is quite diversified as well, but perhaps not in a way that Markowitz would advocate. Stocks in the S&P 500 acquire prominence in the value of the index based on market capitalization: the bigger companies are more important in the index simply because they have a large market capitalization. In an ideal Markowitz portfolio, a stock is in the portfolio because its *pattern of returns* is completely different from any of the other stocks in the portfolio, not because the company has simply grown very large. An S&P 500 index fund is by no means a good illustration of applied portfolio theory.

I can pursue these ideas much more effectively by studying the historical performance of individual stocks, not market index funds or even sector funds. In selecting stocks for a portfolio, since 2008 was such a bad year, an ideal candidate for our portfolio that might have not only held up well in the face of the 2008 selloff, but perhaps even gained in 2008.

The place to start searching for such a company and stock is in the consumer staples area. What companies might continue to do solid business in the face of general and pervasive economic weakness? How, about a company that has been around a long time selling breakfast food to consumers? After all, even in a recession, people continue to eat breakfast food. The company name? General Mills®! General Mills® trades under the ticker symbol GIS. In reality, GIS is a whole lot more than just Cheerios®. It is Haagen Daz® ice cream, Progresso® soup, Pillbury® cake mixes, Totinos® pizza, Hamburger Helper®, Green Giant® vegetables, Youplait® yogurt, and a whole lot more.

What a great company as a core holding in our portfolio to represent the defensive consumer staple sector! All of these General Mills brands are household names. People have to eat even if there is a major recession, and they might stay at home more and even buy more General Mills products if the economy is tanking.

Putting together historical price data on a stock is easy enough, and the NASDAQ Web site compiles this, and adjusts the price to account for stock splits stock as well. The trickier part is that stocks frequently pay dividends, usually once a quarter or four times a year. A stock like General Mills has long been an excellent dividend payer, and the annualized dividend has been running $1.64 per share With a share price of about $50, this works out to a dividend yield of over 3 percent a year, much better than a bank certificate of deposit.

How to treat the dividend becomes an issue in calculating returns. The dividend is taxable income to the shareholder, and the dividend tax rate could vary from 0 percent to 23.8 percent depending on the other income of the shareholder, The dividend could be reinvested in the stock. Not knowing what the income of the shareholder is, I assumed that the dividend will be reinvested in the stock and added that in as part of the return, (the same assumption the funds also make to calculate returns).

The table that follows shows my estimated return to holding GIS stock assuming that none of the annual dividend might be paid out in income taxes. The GIS share prices are the close for December 31 of the year, and a one-time $10,000 purchase of the stock was made at the closing price for Dec 31 of the previous year. In calculating the returns, the NASDAQ historical price data I used accounted for stock splits and for each year I added in the annual reinvested dividend. These numbers may be a bit overstated, but they are close to reality, and approximately comparable to the numbers for mutual funds in the previous two chapters.

	GIS	Price	Gain or Loss	$10,000
	12/31/2007	$28.50	Shares =	350.88
	2008	$30.38	6.60%	$11,239
	2009	$35.41	16.56%	$13,731
	2010	$35.59	0.51%	$14,538
	2011	$40.41	13.54%	$17,327
	2012	$40.42	0.02%	$18,223
	2013	$49.91	23.48%	$23,498

GIS shares year-over-year increased in every year from 2008-2013, and the nice $23,498 end value is in part attributable to the excellent annual dividend yield.

What stock should be the stock representing the health-care sector? Another way to seek out ideas for individual stocks is to "spy" on the mutual fund managers. Periodically, mutual fund managers make public their top-ten holdings. Maybe spy on Fidelity's biotechnology sector portfolio (FBIOX) for an idea of a specific stock the manager there thinks is really good. One big holding is Amgen® (AMGN). Amgen is a biotech company that is bigger and has been around longer than most of the other biotech firms, many of which are smaller and started only recently. Amgen used to not pay any dividend, which is the case or a lot of companies that think of themselves as high-growth, but it began to pay a small dividend starting in 2011. The dividend yield for AMGN is much smaller than for GIS, however.

Amgen has been successful in developing and marketing a host of different biotech products designed to restore heath. As a shareholder, part of the bet you are making is that AMGN will be able to continue to come up with exciting new products and these products will increasingly help a baby-boomer population that will increasingly need them. So Amgen should do well as the population ages.

Here are the comparable data for AMGN.

AMGN	Price	Gain or Loss	$10,000
12/31/2007	$46.44	Shares=	215.33
2008	$57.75	24.35%	$12,435
2009	$56.57	-2.04%	$12,181
2010	$54.90	-2.95%	$11,822
2011	$64.21	16.96%	$13,947
2012	$86.20	34.25%	$19,034
2013	$114.08	32.34%	$25,594

The share price again increased in 2008, like GIS. The shares fell a little in 2009 and 2010, but have taken off since then, giving a nice $25,594 2013 end value counting the reinvested dividends. The profile here from a Harry Markowitz portfolio theory perspective is a very nice pairing with GIS.

Next, I need to identify a stock from the technology sectors. Going to Fidelity Electronics mutual fund, I see that one of their top holdings currently is Intel® (INTC). Intel is the world's leading manufacturer of computer chips for laptop and desktop computers. The fortunes of Intel have been closely tied to those of Microsoft® (MSFT), and a lot of investors see the two companies as much the same kind investment. Intel stumbled in 2008, with shares down over 45 percent. The share price was down nearly 15 percent in 2012 as well. But then 2013 was a strong year, with shares up 25.9 percent.

Why the losses? As the public moved from laptops and into smart phones and tablets, Intel was nowhere to be seen. Apple® was building their own proprietary chips for their iPads® and iPhones®. Other manufacturers of Android tablets and phones were often relying on Chinese-headquartered companies such as Rockchip and Allwinner, neither of which is a household name, but both currently make and sell a lot of chips in Android smart phones and tablets.

Intel is waking up, however. They now are selling a series of chips designed specifically for use in smart phones and tablets. Intel the company has enormous resources, and their serious entry into the smart-phone and tablet market ought to give the smaller companies serious pause. The bet here on Intel the stock is that these new chips will quickly become an important part of a lot of smart phones and tablets. Some of these chips apparently run faster than the chips Apple is using in their products, and that may give even Apple pause. Here are the data for Intel, again a different pattern of returns than for GIS or AMGN.

INTC	Price	Gain or Loss	$10,000
12/31/2007	$26.66	Shares=	375.09
2008	$14.66	-45.01%	$5,704
2009	$20.40	39.15%	$8,148
2010	$21.03	3.09%	$8,636
2011	$24.25	15.31%	$10,251
2012	$20.62	-14.97%	$9,043
2013	$25.96	25.90%	$11,723

The year end 2013 value of $11,723 does not look that attractive, but this stock may be more about the future than the past, and the bet is that Intel will regain its dominance in the chip-making business, this time in tablets and smart phones.

Finally, to complete the four-sector, four-stock portfolio, I need a stock in the energy sector. My candidate for that stock is EOG. EOG is not exactly a household name. It is the oil and gas drilling and production spinoff from the old Enron company, a spinoff completed sometime before Enron the company went bankrupt. Technically EOG are the initials of Enron Oil and gas, although EOG does not like to mention that.

Why is EOG interesting? EOG is responsible for coming up with the combination of oil (and gas) wells with long horizontal segments along with fracturing the organic chemical containing the rock to release the oil or gas. EOG had been successfully doing this for natural gas wells in Texas, and in 2007 decided that it was worth a try to experiment with the same technique to recover crude oil from shale rock that contained crude oil which was all but impossible to recover using any other known method. They decided to try this first on some leases they had acquired cheaply in western North Dakota, and the first well they drilled employing horizontal laterals and fracking was drilled about 3 miles northwest of Parshall North Dakota.

The technique worked, and it worked very well. The EOG share price went up in 2007, but investors still were skeptical. EOG thus began the Bakken oil field in Northwest North Dakota. The state is now the nation's second largest oil producer, with only Texas ahead of them. North Dakota now produces over a million barrels of light sweet crude oil a day, 90 percent from wells employing the lateral and fracking technologies in Bakken shale EOG pioneered starting in late 2006 and early 2007. In addition to EOG, there are now many other oil drillers employing the same techniques to extract crude oil from shale, but EOG was the first. Here are the data for EOG:

EOG	Price	Gain or Loss	$10,000
12/31/2007	$44.63	Shares=	224.06
2008	$33.29	-25.41%	$7,567
2009	$48.65	46.14%	$11,186
2010	$45.71	-6.04%	$10,646
2011	$49.26	7.77%	$11,504
2012	$60.40	22.61%	$14,143
2013	$83.92	38.94%	$19,815

EOG shares dropped off in 2008, but the 25 percent loss that year was far less than the losses for the typical energy-related company. Keep in mind that crude oil prices halved in 2008, before starting to climb again.

So, I now have a portfolio consisting of four interesting stocks. Harry Markowitz would be happy because the sectors each stock represents are largely unrelated, and further, the pattern of gains and losses for each company over time is different. The forces acting on each company are very different. Suppose I am a small investor, and have a total of $10,000 to invest. I divide the $10,000 by putting $2,500 on each stock with these results:

Year	GIS	AMGN	INTC	EOG	Sum
2008	$2,810	$3,109	$1,426	$1,892	$9,236
2009	$3,433	$3,045	$2,037	$2,796	$11,311
2010	$3,634	$2,955	$2,159	$2,662	$11,410
2011	$4,332	$3,487	$2,563	$2,881	$13,263
2012	$4,556	$4,758	$2,261	$3,548	$15,123
2013	$5,874	$6,399	$2,931	$4,970	$20,174

Harry Markowitz would celebrate in that these numbers illustrate very well exactly the principles he taught about constructing a stock portfolio. I sustained a slight loss in 2008 in that my $10,000 total investment is worth $9,236 at the end of 2008, but after that it is all uphill. I am very diversified even with just four stocks, and if something happens to one of the sectors and stocks, chances are all the others will not be adversely affected, or at least not to the same degree. I am also poised for future growth. I more than doubled the $10,000 investment by the end of 2013. Who says a small investor with only a limited funds cannot come up with a good portfolio?

I am by no means advocating that everyone now rush out and buy equal quantities of GIS, AMGN, INTL and EOG as an investment strategy. These stocks merely illustrate how the Markowitz portfolio theory can work using four real stocks and four actual prices. I like how the pattern of returns for energy, health care, technology and consumer staples each usually move in a different way. This makes for a balanced portfolio, and in particular one that will hold up better in a deteriorating market.

Nor am I necessarily saying that a portfolio of individual stocks will work better for most people than, say a portfolio of carefully-selected mutual funds. The mutual fund managers should be cognizant of the same issues I am aware of in constructing the portfolios they manage.

However, a basic advantage of individual stocks for me over funds is that I am not forced to sell my stocks in a market selloff. In the case of the typical mutual fund manager, shareholders redeem a lot of shares when prices drop, and the manager has to liquidate stock to cover the redemptions, even if selling the stock might not be a great idea for the performance of the fund in the longer run. As a shareholder of an individual stock, not only can I decide to not sell a company after a price decrease, but I may even want to purchase *more* shares at bargain prices. Most of the time, the *best strategy* in a market selloff is *not to panic.* Instead, *try and take advantage* of what is happening as events unfold.

The exchange-traded fund GLD directly tracks the price of gold, and is a simple way to invest in gold without having to take delivery on and then store gold coins or bullion. The same numbers are available for GLD as for company stocks. Here are the numbers:

GLD	Price	Gain or Loss	$10,000
12/31/2007	$82.46	Shares=	121.2709
2008	$86.52	4.92%	$10,492
2009	$107.31	24.03%	$13,014
2010	$138.72	29.27%	$16,823
2011	$151.99	9.57%	$18,432
2012	$162.02	6.60%	$19,648
2013	$116.12	-28.33%	$14,082

The gold coin and bullion buyers (the so-called gold *bugs*) were doing quite well through 2012, but then the bottom fell out of the gold market. And the end-of-year 2013 number for GLD is a bit less than for the S&P index fund (14,082 versus 14,290 for the S&P 500 index fund VFINX).

Interestingly, however, the numbers for the metal-based exchange-traded GLD fund look way better than for the Fidelity Precious Metals fund (FSAGX) which invests some of its assets in gold bullion but mainly in stocks of the precious metals miners. I expected GLD and FSAGX to track each other more closely than actually happened over the 6-year period.

Chapter 12

Think Like an Economist!

Economists, particularly applied economists, have a unique way of looking at the world that might seem strange or even a bit weird to other, (normal) people. Nowhere is this better illustrated than in the purchase of depreciating assets.

To illustrate this, consider the purchase of a new vehicle, a 4WD Chevrolet Tahoe with the LT1 trim level. Records indicate that the transaction price on this vehicle new in 2008 was about $36,000, depending in part on whether the new owner ordered the sunroof and the DVD player system or not, as well as the new owner's skills in negotiating the transaction price with the dealer. This number is a good one for our illustration and close to reality in 2008.

Now assume that the new owner drives the vehicle a comparatively-modest 15,000 miles a year, and decides in July of 2014 to trade in the vehicle, now with approximately 90,000 miles on it. The Kelly Blue Book says that the trade-in value on this vehicle, with a DVD player, but no sunroof, is $17,285 if traded to a dealer, or $19,515 if sold to a private party. A realistic number for the value of this vehicle in July of 2014 might be to average these two numbers, since I do not know how the owner plans to dispose of the vehicle. This works out to $18,400.

This means that the total depreciation on the vehicle over the ownership period is $36,000 minus $18,400 equals $17,600, the accumulated depreciation of the vehicle over the ownership period. The vehicle with 90,000 miles on it is currently worth 51 percent of its original purchase price.

It does not take an economist to understand depreciation and that depreciation only part of the costs of vehicle ownership. To depreciation I need to add the costs of insurance, license and registration costs, sales and personal property taxes paid on the vehicle, interest paid if the vehicle was purchased on credit, gasoline, maintenance and repairs. These numbers can add up and cannot be avoided.

But all of these costs are by no means the end of the story. Economists like to use the term *imputed* a lot. There are imputed rents, imputed returns and imputed costs. Economists are constantly thinking about opportunity costs, that is, if the $36,000 had *not* been used to buy the Tahoe, what other things could the money have been used for instead. The *imputed* (sometimes *implicit*) cost of the vehicle ownership includes more than the depreciation and other expense items listed above. Had the vehicle not been purchased, the $36,000 could have been placed in a bank CD over the period, and earned a paltry 2 percent a year compounded. At the end of the 6 ½ year period, the $38,000 would be $40,945 compounded. That number does not seem particularly attractive, but remember to compare it not against the $36,000 purchase price but against the $18,400 depreciated price of the vehicle with 90,000 miles on it.

But instead of putting the $36,000 in a bank CD paying low interest rates, what would the imputed value of the $36,000 be if instead we invested the money in Fidelity Low Priced FLPSX. The value there at the end of 2013 would be $61,355. The investor would have enough to pay cash for a $45,000 vehicle in 2014 for cash plus a $16,355 FLPSX "nest egg" that is still appreciating in value, at least in most years.

The catch with all of this is that most people think they must have a more expensive vehicle than they can afford to buy for cash. They end up taking out an auto loan, which makes the accumulated cost of the vehicle still higher. And then they buy extra doodads on the vehicle that make the kids happy (an $800 DVD player system) but also make the dealership profitable. Once this happens, the real opportunities for building a wealth position go out the window. There is always a better vehicle with more doodads on it out there screaming for attention, which is a major reason why many people are in a poor wealth position.

Applied economists are almost legendary for trying to minimize expenses on assets that always depreciate in value, and love to siphon off money to instead buy assets that have good appreciation potential. A number of applied economists I know truly dreaded going to shopping malls, and avoided them whenever possible. They thought the malls were a huge waste of time. I will go to a shopping mall, I look a lot, but I seldom make any significant purchases. There are usually better and lower-cost alternatives.

A colleague of mine related the story that when he was in graduate school, the economics faculty had something of a contest going on to see who could drive the cheapest, oldest and least reliable vehicle to and from work. A then-famous production economist usually won in that on many nights after work was done he had to locate a group of three or four graduate students to help push-start his car so he could go home. Keep in mind that this was a world-famous economist!

Applied economists are also very good at sizing up odds and probabilities when it comes to risky events, and then backing off in situations where the odds are deemed to be too long.

The casino towns get a major source of their casino business by hosting conventions. But, they also keep close watch on the casino take when each new convention group comes into town. For a group they have never hosted before, the might offer especially good room rates, something that appeals to convention planners.

One year some years back, Reno Nevada won the opportunity to host the AAEA, the Agricultural and Applied Economics Association. The group was excited in part because cheap room prices undercut rates in other non-casino convention towns.

We never heard exactly what the casino take was when we filled several hotels for most of a week that year, except to say that word got back to the association that we never again were going to be invited back. Applied economists do not go in for long-odds gambling. The only group that I can think of that might be worse in this regard for the casino hotels might be an association of applied statisticians, but then it is sometimes difficult to distinguish between an applied economist and an applied statistician anyway, as most applied economists think they are quite good at applied statistics! Applied economists are willing to take risks, but they want the odds to be in their favor!

Chapter 13

Gathering Funds for Investment

Building wealth requires *discipline*, *courage*, and *patience*. All three of these are important, and it is not clear that one of these is more important than the others. Any one of the strategies outlined in the previous chapters could build wealth, but none of them are easy "get rich quick" schemes. This book is not about getting rich in a hurry. It is not a lesson plan for picking numbers on a lottery ticket. This is a book that is all about *Building Wealth Slowly*. If you want a book on how to get rich quickly, this is not it!

Discipline is all about building funds for investment in assets that usually appreciate in value over time. It is less about being fortunate enough to have good luck than it is about setting up the preconditions so that *good luck can happen*.

The non-wealthy complain that the wealthy *have all the good luck*. And there is an element of chance involved, say in picking a stock. But really, becoming wealthy is less about being lucky and more about having discipline.

The non-wealthy frequently claim that they would like to take steps to build a wealth position except that they are *constantly broke*. Being constantly broke is the result of one or two things, alone or together. Either, a person's *income is too low*, or one's *spending on depreciating goods* is too high, or both.

Maybe you think your income is too low in order to buy the things you really want. If so, the only way out of this box is to take the steps necessary to *find a higher-paying job*. The problem here from a wealth-building perspective is that if a person is successful in finding a higher, paying job, then often times this individual thinks that this is a good excuse to *buy still more stuff*. Buying more stuff for these people usually means spending more money on items that will depreciate rapidly in value, items like a new motor vehicle, a boat, or an expensive vacation that was not affordable at the old, lower income, and not on assets that might appreciate in value.

Once again, there is no wealth-building going on in either a new motor vehicle or in a vacation. One needs to prioritize, and in this case it means putting *some emphasis* on *buying and then holding potentially appreciating assets*. If you are focused on using your increased income on items that depreciate, you may think you have improved your daily *standard of living*, but your *wealth position* remains unchanged. Income and wealth are definitely not the same thing.

A second possibility is that your *spending* on depreciating assets is *out of control*. The most important large expenditure on depreciating assets for most people is for motor vehicles. Why do I focus so much on spending for motor vehicles? They asked the famous bank robber Willie Sutton why he chose to rob banks. His response was "because that is where the money is!" In the case of a personal budget, motor vehicles normally represent the single largest discretionary spending item for a rapidly-depreciating asset.

So, people need a vehicle to get to work, run errands and take a vacation. But do you really need two vehicles? And do you need vehicles with heated and cooled seats, a sunroof and leather seats, or would a vehicle with fewer expensive doodads serve you nearly as well? For a lot of people, vehicle-buying is a *vanity purchase* with the vehicle reflecting the personality of the owner rather than a vehicle that has the attributes a person *really needs*. Car dealers love to see this sort of person wander into their dealerships, because they are ideal candidates for the sale of vehicles with lots of high-margin doodads, and selling these high-margin items are what makes the dealership really profitable.

Years ago, people expected vehicles to go for 100,000 miles without a major overhaul. A vehicle was considered pretty much "shot" at 100,000 miles. A lot of people traded for a new vehicle every three years, a costly proposition at best, as the 3-year old vehicle was worth only a fraction of the new purchase price.

Nowadays, motor vehicles go for a lot more miles on average without major repairs. Motor vehicles now go routinely for 150,000 and even 200,000 miles without a major repair. If you can get your head out of the notion that you somehow *must have a new car*, then you can usually make a motor vehicle last a lot longer than you might think. Some people still worry that an older vehicle will more likely leave them stranded on the side of the road, but this is not reality. If this were a common problem you would be seeing lots of stalled older vehicles on the roadsides. Driving motor vehicles for a longer period of time is one potential way of saving money for building wealth.

It is not only the purchase price of the vehicle, it is the numbers of vehicles people somehow think they must own. In addition to depreciation, each vehicle requires care and feeding for items like gasoline, insurance and maintenance. These costs add up. Can you get by with *one less* vehicle and use the money you saved and siphon that into a wealth-building asset?

Another major spending category that needs to be carefully scrutinized is the money spent on items such as vacations and eating out. Some of these items might individually appear to be small, but the costs can quickly add up to some big numbers. Fewer vacations and vacations closer to home may mean fewer miles on a motor vehicle. Fewer meals eaten out might improve family relationships and be healthier for the family members as well. Each of these items needs to be carefully scrutinized from the perspective of being happy with less.

A lot of men resolve issues relating to their *wives not wanting to cook meals all the time* by simply taking everyone out to eat. A better strategy might be for the man to take over the cooking tasks on a frequent basis. Some guys seem to think they are just way *too masculine* to learn how to cook and share cooking responsibilities. They are willing to make steaks or burgers on the gas grill outdoors, but working an electronic range is beyond (or perhaps beneath) them. This is sad.

Maybe the entire family would be better off with *shared* cooking responsibilities and largely home-made not restaurant meals. While the man is learning, the kids (*both* the girls *and* the boys) can learn cooking techniques at the same time. (How is that for equality of the sexes?) This is also an opportunity for kids to learn about different foods, and more importantly, to learn to love foods they do not serve over the counter at McDonalds®!

Gathering Funds for Investment

Another major set of spending items that need to be carefully scrutinized are regular monthly expenditures for a host of different items. Take a look at your cable TV bill. Take a look at your cell phone bill(s), land line bills, and for that matter, any service for which there is a regular monthly charge. Is all of this *really necessary* in order to function on a daily basis, or is some of it simply frills that could be cut without doing serious damage to your lifestyle?

Finally, look in the shopping cart. A recent estimate is that a family of four should spend no more than $180 a month on groceries, and this assumes that they will be eating only a meal a week out. This works out to $45 a person, on average. If your spending is running significantly higher than that, how come?

One problem is that a lot of people go into a grocery store with very specific ideas about what they want to buy and eat that week. A better strategy is to see what the grocery store has on sale that week. A lot of money can be saved at the meat counter simply by adjusting one's menu for the week to what meats happen to be a really good buy. Then load up on items on sale like potatoes that will last more than a week.

Maybe you do not need to buy the expensive *rib eye steaks*. A basic problem with rib eyes are that they taste good but are loaded with saturated animal fat. A sirloin steak is not only far cheaper, it not only tastes good on the grille, but is much better for your waistline and your health. For some odd reason, a lot of people do not think like this. I am a big advocate of the idea that when it comes to food, kids need to learn to love leaner, healthier alternatives. I like food alternatives that not only taste good but are good for the waistline!

And what about the store brands as a cheaper alternative to the national brands? Store brands for a host of different grocery items have improved to the point that they are indistinguishable from the national brands. The only time I buy national brands is if they are on sale at a price as cheap or cheaper than the store brand. And as a real money-saving strategy, I look for *store brands* on sale, and then load up.

Then there is the shopping at discount stores and department stores. Carefully examine the items your shopping cart. Do you really *need* all of that? For goodness sakes, why? Are there items in the cart that you could do just as well without? Each item seems individually like a small expense, but together the stuff you are buying but do not really need can quickly add up. This is where potentially-investible assets are turning into depreciating assets. We need to change this.

Some people are fascinated by department stores and in particular, name brands. They think that buying clothing at a discount store like a Walmart® or a Kmart® is somehow *beneath them*. And, for goodness sakes shopping at a clothing retailer like TJMaxx® is just way beneath them. Being brand-conscious when it comes to clothing is an excellent want to spend way too much money on clothing.

A key to building wealth is to develop the discipline to pursue paths that others for whatever reason seem to be avoiding. A lot of these paths involve diverting spending on various depreciating items with an eye toward building a fund to invest in appreciating assets.

Let me assume that you have developed the *discipline* to build a fund for investment by reducing your consumption of depreciating items such as motor vehicles, vacations, meals eaten out and spending at the mall and the grocery, discount and department stores. The next step is to have the *courage* to do something that could lead to an increasing wealth.

People differ in their ability to handle risk. The investible assets *could be placed* in a federally-insured bank certificate of deposit. The money is "safe" there. People build savings with bank deposits, but no one ever built wealth in doing so.

Building wealth is all about getting the *courage* to invest the money in something that is *not risk-free*. The wolves are everywhere. You could use the funds to buy lottery tickets, but the odds of even getting your money back, let alone making money on that "investment" are so low that for all practical purposes they are zero. You could put the money in a slot machine at a casino, also with terrible odds of winning.

A basic problem is that a lot of people, risk-wise, fail to distinguish between slot-machine odds and odds in the stock market. These same people tend to gravitate toward individual cheap but high-risk stocks, stocks that could have, but are unlikely to have, a big payoff. Note that in the chapter dealing with investing in individual stocks, I avoided making investments in small startup companies. None of the companies I picked is in any real danger of going bankrupt. I admit that there are sections of the stock market that look a lot like odds at a slot machine, but having the outlook of a casino gambler generally is not a good strategy for building wealth.

A share of General Mills is not at all the same thing, risk-wise. General Mills makes an array of items people buy and eat every week. The possibility of General Mills ever going bankrupt is all but zero. The only question is not "will the company go bankrupt?" but rather "how fast will it be able to grow over a five- or ten-year period?"

There are riskier bets in my portfolio, but I believe these are all *reasonable* bets. Will EOG continue to consistently strike a lot of oil over the next 5 or 10 years? Will Amgen continue to be successful in coming up with new therapies that cure disease? Will Intel be successful in building and selling computer chips outside their traditional areas of laptop and desktop computers? Are they smart enough to compete successfully in smart phone and tablet chips against both market leader Apple and the cheap Chinese-headquartered chipmakers?

None of this is certain, but each of these seems to be a *reasonable*, not a *long-odds* bet. Are you willing to place some of that money you siphoned off from spending on depreciating assets in order to test this all out? Maybe the expensive vacation was a better idea, but this is where *courage* comes in for building wealth. Having *courage* is one thing: having the *right kind of courage* is another, far rarer attribute. There are far more lottery-ticket buyers than there are serious investors.

The third attribute is *patience*. I see a lot of potential investors that seem to have the investor-equivalent of about a ten-minute attention span. They buy a stock and then get agitated and uneasy if the share price initially goes down not up. They are super scared of losses, even if the losses are only on paper. People who lack patience tend to trade a lot of stocks. They never simply sit back on their earlier decisions and wait for events to gel.

Generally speaking, being overly-concerned about short-term share-price movements leads to a situation where the investor ends up buying at high prices and selling at low prices. Maybe a better strategy is to instead simply sit tight in the face of a selloff, or more aggressively, buy even more if the price gets really cheap. One needs to examine the specific reasons why the share price is declining. Companies usually report quarterly earnings, and not every quarter is going to be better than the last. Many stock market *traders* pay close attention to short-term price movements as a consequences of a unusually bad (or good) quarter. If the share price drops, they cannot resist the urge to sell. If the share price rises, they cannot resist the urge to buy. This leads to large *intraday volatility* in share prices.

This also is exactly the *wrong* buy or sell strategy. The proper strategy is to buy when shares are cheap and (perhaps) sell if there is a large price increase that might not persist. You are doing the opposite of what the dumb traders are doing. But remember, the traders you are up against usually have a 10-minute attention span, and their selling can set up opportunities for the rest of us with a bit more *patience* to get a stock at a very good price and simply *hold* the stock for the long term (maybe five years, ten years or even longer). One basic principle is that stock investing might be even more about *when* you buy than about *what* you buy. Patience oftentimes is more about just hanging in there than about being a clairvoyant with respect to what the stock price will be in the immediate future.

Successful people at building wealth are *disciplined* with respect to how they spend their money, have the *courage* to take on reasonable risks, and the *patience* to pursue long-term goals even if events turn against them in the shorter-run. Those who lack these wealth-building skills tend to believe that income is the most important factor in determining wealth, are careless in their money-spending habits, gravitating toward making purchases that depreciate rapidly in value as opposed to appreciating assets, and often believe that wealthy people got where they are not because of their own money-management skills but because of dumb luck. For them, becoming wealthy is not unlike winning the lottery, with similar long odds.

Chapter 14

What Every Boy and Girl (Adults Too!) Should Know

Successful money management that leads to long-term wealth building is no simple task, and requires a combination of discipline, courage and patience. Children with parents who lack these financial skills frequently grow into adulthood lacking these same skills themselves.

If the parents lack these basic financial management skills, who is to teach them? There is usually no class in grade school or high school that deals with the issues involved, issues that include human psychology with respect to topics such as owning stuff, the merits of saving for the future versus spending now, and the nuances of taking reasonable but not undue risks when making choices when future outcomes are uncertain.

I think it is reasonable for even grade school kids to learn that

1. *A dollar that is spent today on something you want (a depreciating asset) is a dollar that you will never ever get to spend again.* Once whatever you bought wears out or is gone, you can never ever get the dollar back. This same thing applies to eating hamburgers, clothing, toys, carnival rides, motor vehicles and

anything that will be worth less or nothing tomorrow than it is worth today.

2. *A dollar spent on a potentially-appreciating asset could easily turn into more dollars at some future point in time.* A dollar not spent on a depreciating asset could turn into $2 (or a whole lot more) in, say a college fund. One reason so many students are in deep debt for college is because their parents were all hung up on giving their kids things right now as opposed to investing in their future.

I love to watch old episodes of "Leave it to Beaver" on MeTV. What fascinates me the most are certain cultural elements that have somehow gotten lost in America since the series was filmed. The series was filmed in the late 1950s and early 1960s.

Wally and Beaver mention getting a "weekly allowance" from their parents, and then regularly get into some financial scrape that their allowance cannot quite cover. Dad is always reluctant to bail the kids out of the scrape by just giving them money but sometimes strikes a deal to cover the crisis with the expectation that Wally and Beaver will pay dad back over time with funds coming from their weekly allowance.

How many parents think in these terms anymore? This is all about teaching kids the financial consequences of being responsible for their own financial decisions, good or bad. Nowadays, if a kid gets into a financial problem, the parent is expected to bail the kid out immediately, with no repayment terms.

Allowances themselves have gone out of favor. With an allowance, a child can start to learn about the basics of financial management, learning that a dollar spent today is

What Every Boy and Girl (Adults Too) Should Know

a dollar that can never be re-spent at some future point in time and that in buying something big might require saving a portion of one's allowance for weeks or even months.

Nowadays, most children seem to just tell their parents what they want and the parents are somehow expected to just cough up the cash to buy whatever it is. Kids quickly become adept at understanding that the only thing they need to do to get something is to tell their parents what it is, and it will appear almost like magic. As these kids grow a little older, they frequently try the same stunt on others, other relatives, for example. The basics involved in learning how to defer consumption are lost.

As adults, these same individuals believe that if they want something, the government should pay for it. Why work to get something if there is a strategy that involves using someone else's money instead? This, in turn, leads to a society filled with potential free-loaders who are ignorant about financial planning. My parents never taught me how to do this, so why should the rules I operate with as an adult be any different?

In an episode of "Leave it to Beaver, originally aired June 23, 1962, (imdb.com) dad decides to teach Wally and Beaver about the stock market by giving them $100 to invest. Dad suggests a stable but staid utility stock, but Wally's buddy Eddie Haskell thinks the boys should buy a high-tech but risky stock related to the space program. The buys buy the stock Eddie suggested, an at first it rises dramatically, but then suddenly drops to a fraction of the purchase price. The episode concludes with dad being the hero, admitting he had his broker sell the boys out of the stock just before it fell off the edge.

One of the basic lessons of this book is that people of all ages, young and old, need to be responsible for the consequences of their own decisions whether they turn out right or wrong, good or bad. It is simply not fair to go through life complaining that someone or something else was to blame when in fact what happened that you did not like was a direct result of your own decisions. Episodes of "Leave it to Beaver" nearly always end with the boys learning how to accept and then deal with the consequences of decisions that were theirs alone regardless of the outcome. Occasionally, dad will bail Beaver or Wally out of a predicament one of the two created for himself, but only after the life-lesson is learned.

Some people seem to think that such an approach is antiquated: I believe otherwise. Children need to be taught at an early age that each person is responsible for the consequences of the decisions that each person makes, and dealing with the consequences of what turned out to be a bad decision is an important part of becoming a mature adult.

There is no clearer example of all of this than in the decisions made by young people to "buy stuff". Sadly, many children nowadays grow up in homes where the only thing they have to do to get stuff is to put on an act for their parents with respect to how badly they *need* something. Parents frequently have some major hang-ups too. Some parents seem to believe that parenting involves giving their kids everything the parents did not have as a kid themselves. If a child wants something, that is all that matters!

If the parents feel that their primary obligation somehow is to give their kids everything that the parents did not have when they were their age, then the parents are on a dangerous track as well. This is a major cause of overspending and a financial plan that places little, if any, emphasis on what might happen in the future. It is all about having fun with things you can buy today, not about what could happen or be possible in the future. Not surprisingly, many of these parents are deep in credit-card and other short-term debt as well.

For the children, these issues extend right into adulthood. The child who always got stuff just by begging the parents for it quickly becomes the adult who cannot do any sort of long-term financial planning, and these children not wanting to have to forgo anything, quickly end up loaded down with car loan and other short term debt. *If my parents never did any longer-term financial planning, then why should I?* Teens who never were forced to work in order to get money to buy anything they wanted become adults who keep hitting up their parents for the extra money to support the depreciating assets lifestyle they simply cannot afford on the income they have.

I am not normally in favor of parents giving adult children money to just to support a lifestyle they cannot afford on their own. I might make an exception on this if there were a truly unforeseen family crisis, but a family crisis is not about funding a new car or, for that matter, a Disney World® vacation! *Learning how to live within one's means and income is the most important life lesson of all. Bettering oneself is all about taking the necessary steps to improve one's life.*

I think that young people need the opportunity to manage money on their own. A more interesting proposition would be to let the teen-and-older children hone their skills in money management by providing an "investment fund" in which the children get the opportunity to make real decisions not only what to spend now versus later, and in particular, how to manage money with an eye toward wealth creation as a goal. The issue with this, of course, is that it is always easier to invest money if it is not yours.

There is no substitute to actually seeing the value of your own investment both rise *and* fall, and part of the entire experience is having *your own money*, not your parent's money, at stake! Parents who do poorly at longer-term financial management often create kids who also lack the same necessary long-term planning skills. Children learn from their parents in a whole lot of different ways!

I am all in favor of converting every child into a *financially-responsible* adult, and this will never happen so long as parents are convinced that their position in life requires that they simply *give* their children practically everything they want. Children need to learn that if they are going to have stuff, they need to take the necessary steps to get the money they need on their own, and that any money that is spent on assets that depreciate will never get to be spent again at some future point in time. Finally, they need to learn to derive satisfaction not from acquiring lots of stuff, but merely by seeing if through careful investing, one dollar can somehow be made into two dollars at some future point in time.

Chapter 15

America, the Beautiful

O beautiful for spacious skies,
For amber waves of grain,
For purple mountain majesties
Above the fruited plain!
America! America! God shed His grace on thee,
And crown thy good with brotherhood
From sea to shining sea!—Katherine Lee Bates

America truly is the land of opportunity! A lot of people like to complain a lot that somehow opportunities have missed them. Then they look for someone else to bail them out of whatever financial predicament that they have gotten themselves into, maybe a parent or relative, or even the US government.

I do not see it that way at all, and I am always happiest when I can map a strategy of my own that does not rely on anyone else or any other entity for financial assistance. Some people seem to think that they can build wealth simply by buying at the local auto dealership or the local discount or department store. The basic problem with that strategy is that none of these places have ever sold anything that has any chance of appreciating in value: these businesses are all about selling assets that will surely depreciate. If motor vehicles lasted forever, auto dealers would be out of business! More generally, if the stuff people buy at discount houses lasted forever, the shopping carts at Target® would all be empty.

Some people seem to think that other people, not them, have all the *good luck*. These same people line up to buy lottery tickets or spend time at a slot machine in a casino, hoping against hope that they too will somehow have good luck happen to them as well, in spite of almost impossibly-low odds.

If you see life in America as being a big game to see who can own the most expensive consumer goods (depreciating assets), then you are going in with a completely wrong attitude, and you are never going to be able to accumulate wealth. The wealthy are not smarter or luckier than the rest of us: mostly, they simply set their priorities differently with respect to how they *spend* the money they have.

I do not like long odds: I have never bought a lottery ticket. On the other hand, I have always been anxious to map a strategy that has *some* risk, but sets up the preconditions whereby *good luck can happen to me*. I suppose a big lottery-ticket winner may say that he or she would have never won the lottery if the ticket had not been purchased, but this was still 99.99999 percent chance of losing.

I do not like to pursue strategies that are perfectly safe, either. Some people are so concerned about losing money that they never try *anything* beyond putting money in a bank certificate of deposit. I am all in favor of holding sufficient cash to be able to deal with emergencies, but if you muddle through life with all of your funds in cash, you miss out on a whole lot of the very best America has to offer. Holding *only* cash in a bank account is another way of ensuring that *good luck will never shine*.

Nor am I a gold bug. Let me suppose that the economy is on the verge of collapsing. Would I expect that a gold coin that sold for $1,200 is somehow a better investment than 60 shares of General Mills (GIS) that sold for $50 a share? Surely the GIS share value could drop, but in the face of a general economic collapse, do you really think there will still be people so anxious to hold gold rather than to eat that they are willing to bid up the price of gold even as the GIS shares decline in value?

If I am hungry, I would much rather have a Pillsbury brownie mix than a gold coin! The argument that gold prices will keep going up in the face of impending economic collapse holds no weight with me.

My entire life has been most interesting. I will leave it for you to judge whether or not I simply have had tremendously good luck and whether I owe everything to the willingness of others to support me, financially and otherwise, or whether I actually took steps all along the way to make it possible for good luck to shine on me.

Throughout my adult life I have always prided myself in *not* having to rely on my family for financial assistance to do anything I wanted to do. So, given that, how did I manage to make things happen?

In retrospect, my family was poor. I grew up in a house with under 600 square feet that lacked even indoor plumbing. The funny part is that I never thought of myself as being poor. Maybe this was a real key to my subsequent success. I graduated from high school as an honor student, and by the time I was a senior I had collected enough scholarships to begin college at North Dakota State University in Fargo (NDSU).

I had an amazingly good life at NDSU. I just loved it! People were throwing scholarship money at me right and left, and I somehow managed to get ranked first or second in the entire NDSU class every year I was there. By that time, I had managed to accumulate enough money from various scholarships such that I had accumulated about $1,000 in "excess scholarship money." My parents did not pay for any of this college education, and I was debt-free by my senior year, indeed, more than debt free.

In my first three years of college I went without a car. My expenses were low. By the time I was a senior I had already accumulated over a thousand dollars in "excess scholarship money" that I had in the bank, and went off to Rensch Garage in Makoti, ND to buy myself a brand-new 1969 Camaro (at that point in time I was not even aware that I could perhaps make a killing in GIS stock!).

So, I told Rensch's that I wanted the same finance deal they do for farmers, that is, three payments on the Camaro, one in each fall. I would give him $1,000 now and the rest would be financed with three $800 annual payments. He said "we normally only do those deals for farmers. What is your source of income? I said, well I raise these sheep on the farm, and I have a $3,000 Phi Kappa Phi fellowship for my Masters work at NDSU. (After all, I had managed to graduate from NDSU ranked number 1 in the entire senior class, but Jerry seemed unimpressed!) I could tell that Jerry Rensch thought those income sources were pretty paltry, but somehow he went along with the scheme. The sheep did well, they had lots of lambs, and my expenses as a Master's student at NDSU were minimal.

I rented a room at the then department chair's house (Fred Taylor), and I think the rent was $50 a month. Then I took a food contract at the Student Union. I suspect that my total expenses were under $1,500 for the entire year.

Perhaps half of the remainder of the $3,000 ended up getting paid on the new car. I do not remember exactly when I finished paying off the rest of the car, but it was in less than the planned three years.

I was rooming at Fred Taylors' house and one morning I woke up to a phone call from Lu Eisgruber, (a then key faculty member in the Purdue Agricultural Economics department), offering me a special high-end fellowship from Purdue that paid more money than a standard assistantship as well as spend all my time concentrating on my course work and research without having to do time-consuming things like grading papers for professors. The rate was $5,500. Not only would I would be earning about $1,500 more than most graduate assistants were earning, the pay was not that different from the base pay rate for a beginning school teacher.

Graduate fellowship money has other key advantages. For starters, it was completely free of income taxes at both the state and federal level, whereas teaching was often subject to pesky income taxes. I am never one to walk away from a deal that looks good financially. After Lu Eisgruber got off the phone I quickly called my parents to announce that I was probably going to go to Purdue rather than Iowa State, which had not yet made an offer.

Mom fretted a bit but did not tell me I could not do that. She thought West Lafayette was a long way from Parshall, North Dakota. I assured her that if the 1969 Camaro could get to Ames, Iowa, it could probably make its way across Illinois and get to West Lafayette, Indiana, as well, and Indiana soon became my adopted state. In retrospect this was the right decision.

The good things happened for me in large measure because I made them happen for myself. When I wanted to do something that I thought might further my situation, my parents let me do it without complaining, and I was always grateful for that. But I also never asked my parents or any other family member to partly- or entirely-fund a scheme I had in mind to do, this whether it was going to graduate school, buying a house or car or whatever I happened to be working on for a strategy at the moment. I always was given the opportunity to proceed, but no one volunteered to pay for something I was trying to do.

Part of my obligation was to identify a way to make whatever it was happen without relying on anyone else. I am grateful for that too. I ended up smarter and wiser. I probably made a few mistakes along the way, but the consequences never put a financial burden on anyone else. So far as I was concerned, that was a basic requirement.

I was off to Purdue for a doctorate, earning big bucks ($5,500 a year), and my expenses were a bit more than they were at NDSU but not by that much. I think I paid off the rest of what I owed on the Camaro that winter in 1970-71. I do not recall ever making more than one more payment on the car. Jerry Rensch was happy as he had my money, and I had my 1969 Camaro!

In retrospect, the new cars were cheap at that point in time too. Plus, there were schemes at Purdue for making more money on-the-side. I remember teaching an introductory agricultural economics course for a couple years, all for extra pay.

I also came out of Purdue in with a freshly-minted doctorate, completely debt free, and I still recall having a nice savings account at the bank with at least a couple thousand dollars tucked away on the day I finished my PhD. I was offered and accepted a job as an assistant professor at the University of Kentucky at the (then phenomenal) annual wage rate of $16,500. My expenses were higher, as my new townhouse/apartment was $210 a month. I was in that apartment until 1976, and my parents visited me in that apartment at least a couple of times.

In January of 1976, I happened to notice a builder was building neat one-story ranch homes near my apartment with 1,600 sq ft and a two-car garage and a big 80-foot wide lot for $43,800. That was a neat property for that money, but the builder wanted 20-percent down. Basically, counting the closing costs, they wanted $10,000 up front in order to qualify for the 30-year, 7 ½ percent mortgage. I took a look at my bank balance and decided in January that I only had $8,000 in January, 1976. But, given my frugal spending habits (the 69 Camaro was fully paid for years ago, for goodness sakes) I would easily have $10,000 saved to pay down on the house by August 1, when the builder was going to be done building it.

The monthly payments on the new house were going to be $307, but that included the escrow for the property tax, and in the early years of a mortgage the payment was mostly either interest or property taxes, so these could be deducted from my federal and state income taxes. The net after-tax cost per month was probably $250 (versus $210 for the apartment) but no more than that. Inflation rates were rising, and houses in Lexington were going up even faster. The builder was offering the same house as mine the day I moved in at about $49,000—not the $43,800 I contracted to pay the day I moved in, so I already had substantial appreciation in the value by the day I took possession of the new house.

My parents came to visit at my first house many times practically every October. Sometimes they flew down, but they really loved the passenger train. Once they took the train to Louisville. That turned into a real adventure getting home, and, after that, they went back to flying. Even though mom was apprehensive about me buying the house, she absolutely loved it. She could not understand why I would ever want to leave it, but there is a footnote to that story. On these trips, we also ate lots and lots of fish at Captain D's®, something I still do with abandon.

By the following spring, April, 1977, I was getting consulting contracts that needed to be done in Indianapolis, 200 miles away, and I was starting to worry that the 69 Camaro was now 8-years old and may not be up to the task of driving back and forth so much, especially on snowy roads. It had gone through several water pumps at $40 a pop and I had the service station put in a new dimmer switch , but they only charged me about $3.

So I went down to the local Chevy dealer and found a bright metallic red (called *firethorn red*) 1977 Camaro for $5,600. Having just made the $10,000 down payment on the house, I was pretty broke, so I paid about $2,000 down and took out a car loan for $3,600 with monthly payments. I was still accumulating cash, and quickly got tired of messing with paying the loan via monthly payments, and so I think I paid the balance off in the summer of 1978. The loan on the red '77 Camaro was the last auto loan I have ever had.

The consulting contracts paid pretty well, typically $300-$500 a day, plus I was still earning my full salary at the University of Kentucky. UK has a policy that permits each faculty member to have 44 working-days of paid consulting. A quick calculation means that I could all but double my salary with consulting work. I brought home $10,000 in consulting checks alongside my university salary, but I was still saving money from my UK salary.

I did a bunch of interesting stuff with some of the money I earned during my consulting years.

To illustrate, my parents had a little refrigerator dating from maybe the very early 50s. In later years it sat in the entryway as a spare refrigerator. I decided my parents needed a new refrigerator as a Christmas present in 1978 or 1979, and I could easily afford to buy them one. I had just gotten the new Sears Christmas catalog and there was a big new frost-free refrigerator for $479. Further, they could deliver it free to Minot. So I ordered the refrigerator out of the catalog and had it delivered to Minot, whereupon dad drove the pickup over there and brought it home. Mom was delighted!

In the early 80s I found myself with some extra money from one of my consulting projects I had worked on, about $3,000. I could have spent that on another car, after all, I was driving 200 miles back and forth to Indianapolis on a regular basis. Instead, I decided to try out the new-fangled IRA, which meant that the money would accumulate on a tax deferred basis. I did the same thing for a couple more years, and ended up with an investment of about $8,000 total.

The tricky part is that I could not get the money back without paying a big penalty before I reached 59 ½. At that point 59 ½ seemed a long ways away. Then the federal rules on who could and could not invest in an IRA changed, and I could no longer do this. I am not complaining because I got new options for investing spare cash in a retirement account through my university employment, and that worked out well too.

So, the $8,000 sat there with me just watching it and occasionally making changes in investments as the market moved sometimes up and sometimes down. I did my best but sometimes I admit I messed up the management of the IRA. As of last night, that $8000 is now worth $236,000. Never mind the mess-ups. The shiny car would have been in the junk yard long ago. Now I can afford to buy a really shiny car, maybe something costing $150,000 after I pay the taxes on the IRA. I could do that without batting an eye, but it might be even more fun to see if I can turn the $236,000 into $500,000. That should be comparatively easy given that I only have to double my money, when I have already accomplished many times that. The shiny car and the purchase of depreciating assets with the money becomes a distraction to the really fun part. The $150,000 car will only depreciate in value, and fast! Am I somehow suffering because I did not get to spend the $8000 on assets that depreciate in value? You can answer that question for me.

Since 1964, The University of Kentucky has what is called a defined-contribution retirement program for its faculty and staff, a program in which the employee not the University makes the decision with respect to how the money is invested over the long term. As a consequence, the income a new retiree receives is not guaranteed, but rather will depend on how successful the employee was at managing the money. In the case of the University of Kentucky, for faculty, the faculty member pays 5 percent of the annual salary tax-deferred into the retirement program, and the University matches that with with a 10-percent contribution.

These numbers seem high by the standards of corporate America, where an even-match 5-percent 401(k) plan would be considered generous, but a University faculty member normally does not earn a salary anywhere near the salary of a corporate employee either, and the retirement plan is one of the key "perks" of working at a good university.

Defined-contribution programs scare the socks off of some people. Labor unions hate them, and think that employees should be simply guaranteed a fixed income in retirement, fully paid for by the company they were employed. Many states provide retirement plans for employees of the state, only to discover that the incomes promised cannot be supported by the value of the funds the state has in the plan.

In the case of a defined-contribution plan, since the annual retirement income is not guaranteed, the employee not the employer or state takes the risk associated with the up-and-down movement in the stock-and-bond markets.

In a defined-contribution plan, the upside potential is unlimited, but so is the downside. Not having a guaranteed retirement income no matter what with a defined-contribution plan bothers a lot of people.

When I started work at the University of Kentucky, there were only two options to choose from in the retirement plan, TIAA, which was backed by bonds, and guaranteed a minimum interest rate, and a single option in CREF, which was essentially a diversified stock mutual fund. Employees could put all their retirement money in one or the other, or in various percentages, most often 50-percent TIAA and 50-percent CREF.

To try to avoid the stock market risk, an employee could choose to, say, put 75 percent in TIAA and 25 percent in CREF. A riskier strategy with better upside potential might be 25-percent TIAA and 75-percent CREF. The riskiest strategy, but the strategy with the best long-term upside potential was 100-percent CREF, with all the retirement funds invested in the stock market. Further, employees could move money back and forth between the options, accumulated money, new contributions, or both.

Being 26-years old then and something of a risk-taker even back then, and seeking long-term capital appreciation in a situation where I did not expect to tap into my retirement funds for a long time, I opted to go 100-percent CREF. I stuck with that strategy throughout my entire years of employment. About 20 years later, my mom learned that I was still opting to go for 100-percent CREF. Mom said "I don't like it that you have all your money for retirement riding in the stock market"

My response was "But mom, I have been doing this for twenty years!"

I got seriously interested in investing in stock mutual funds with non-retirement money about 1980 as well, starting with diversified actively-managed mutual funds, then moving on to experimenting with sector funds starting in the 1990s, following with investment strategies employing individual stocks.

The real estate market in Lexington, Kentucky has always been very stable, seldom declining substantially but never getting away from itself on the upside, either. I sold the house I purchased in 1976 for $43,800 for about twice what I paid for it in 1994, or $92,000. I used the appreciation plus some of the money I had accumulated in cash to purchase a larger home in a more upscale neighborhood closer to the University for $174,000. That house has since also doubled in value or more.

In 1994, I also paid cash for a small house on a half-acre lot in Plaza North Dakota, a small town where few people at that time wanted to live. I paid $21,000 for it. My parents moved into it and lived there till the year 2000, when my dad died and my mom moved into a nursing home. That house is now at the edge of the Bakken oil boom, a boom which has brought an influx of people looking for housing. I still have that house. No telling what it is worth except to say whatever the value is, the number is a lot higher than $21,000, so houses as appreciating assets have treated me well.

I currently own four motor vehicles, the newest being a 2008 model. Two are collector cars., the original 1969 Camaro in North Dakota, and a 1965 Chevy II Nova here in Lexington, Kentucky. I bought the Nova for $1,600 in 1989, and spent another $2,000 in paint and restoration items. The 1995 Sebring is still my "daily driver" here in Lexington. The 2008 Pontiac Grand Prix (a former Las Vegas rental car) in North Dakota was purchased (for $12,500, approximately half the new price) in the spring of 2009, and, now with 35,000 miles, it is my daily driver when I am in North Dakota. So, I have quite a few cars, but my expenditures on all of them in total are quite low.

Have I somehow missed out on life because of my decisions and choices for spending money? I do not think so, and, if confronted with the same options once more, I have few, if any regrets. But that is ultimately for you to decide.

This book has focused a lot on the importance of *discipline* in building an asset base for investment, *courage* in making investments even when outcomes may be uncertain, and *patience* in sticking with your choices even though events may sometimes turn against you in the short run. This is all about developing *confidence* in your own ability to make choices that defer current consumption in search of future gains, and in your ability to make wise choices with large payoffs over the longer term.

Maybe there is an even better word to summarize all of this. That word is *determination*. If I were to summarize what makes the wealthy different from the non-wealthy, I could sum it all up by saying that the wealthy invariably have a lot of *determination*, and that this *determination* includes a combination of all that is embodied in the words *discipline, courage, patience* and *confidence*.

www.ingramcontent.com/pod-product-compliance
Lightning Source LLC
Chambersburg PA
CBHW051537170526
45165CB00002B/772